BEARING WITNESS

"A book rich in heart and keen in wisdom. Perhaps no Western spiritual master has done more to bridge the chasm between the life of contemplation and the life of action than Bernie Glassman. What he has to teach us is invaluable, if only for the way he continually underlines the connection between spiritual practice and service: enlightenment does not exist in a vacuum. Bernie's simple stories often brought tears to my eyes. He paints his scenes in a few deft strokes, like a master calligrapher, often delivering a sharp, poignant image with very little excess verbiage. Bernie Glassman's ultimate act of service may be to compel us to question our own comfort with the status quo, both material and spiritual, to jettison our own preconceptions, and take the plunge into the unknown."

—Peter Occhiogrosso, *Yoga Journal*

"This bracing and hope-filled book can change your life. Without a shred of pomposity, it redefines the spiritual challenge facing us all. Its real-life stories show us how to be simply, radically present to our suffering world, without pretending to have the answers. And they show the healing, for all concerned, that arises from that plain act of courage."

—Joanna Macy

"A spirituality of hope, against all odds. Bernie Glassman's wise and astonishing book takes us to the verge of our tormented world. He is like a guide through Dante's inferno, showing us that hell on earth need not be our destiny."

—Daniel Berrigan, S.J.

"A remarkable book of 'right action.' A must for those who wish to ground their growth, to become real, to act from their true heart."

—Stephen Levine

By the same author (with Rick Fields)

Instructions to the Cook:
A Zen Master's Lessons in Living a Life That Matters

Bernie Glassman's birthday retreat outside the Capitol in Washington, D.C., 1994.

BEARING WITNESS

A Zen Master's Lessons
in Making Peace

BERNIE GLASSMAN

With Photographs by Peter Cunningham

BELL TOWER
NEW YORK

Published by Bell Tower, an imprint of
Harmony Books,
a division of Crown Publishers, Inc.,
201 East 50th Street, New York, New York 10022.
Member of the Crown Publishing Group.

Originally published in hardcover by
Bell Tower in 1998.
First paperback edition published in 1999.

Random House, Inc. New York, Toronto, London,
Sydney, Auckland
www.randomhouse.com

Bell Tower and colophon are registered trademarks of
Random House, Inc.

Printed in the United States of America

Design by June Bennett-Tantillo

Library of Congress Cataloging-in-Publication Data

Glassman, Bernard (Bernard Tetsugen)
Bearing witness : a Zen master's lessons in
making peace / Bernie Glassman.
p.   cm.
1. Peace—Religious aspects—Zen Buddhism.
2. Spiritual life—Zen Buddhism.
3. Zen Buddhism—Doctrines.   4. Auschwitz
(Concentration camp)   I. Title.
BQ4570.P4G53   1998
294.3'37873—dc21   97-41294

ISBN 0-609-80391-3

10 9 8 7 6 5 4 3 2 1

First Paperback Edition

To the inhabitants of the Letten and the streets,
to the souls of Auschwitz-Birkenau,
and to all peacemakers in the Ten Directions,
past, present, and future.

CONTENTS

CONTENTS

ACKNOWLEDGMENTS

I would like to express my deep appreciation to those who represent the direct karma streams of this book. First and foremost, its words and images are the manifestations of Eve Marko, a founding member of the order. The writing of this book was a six-month-long private time of study between her and me. Working with me, she put my vision and teachings into a form conveying the deep subtlety and ordinariness of Zen and Life, which are, after all, one and the same.

My wife, Jishu Holmes, cofounder of the Zen Peacemaker Order, was responsible for many of the birthings described in these chapters and made important comments on the contents. I also thank Grover Gauntt, executive director of the order, for his extensive review and edit of the manuscript.

This book comes to the reader through the bodies and minds of people throughout space and time. It comes together like a peacemaker robe, with one weaver and the numerous threads of many lives. I wish to thank peacemaker priests Joan Halifax, Fleet Maull, Claude Thomas, and other members and associates of the Zen Peacemaker Order for the stories that are woven here.

PROLOGUE

On January 18, 1994, I celebrated my fifty-fifth birthday by throwing myself a party. I held my party outdoors in the snow on the steps of the U.S. Capitol. There, wrapped in a coat and a blanket, I sat the entire day with one question in mind: What can I do about homelessness, AIDS, and violence in this country?

Sometimes there were fifteen people at my party, other times as many as thirty. It lasted five days. As things turned out, the days we sat outside on the steps of the Capitol were some of the coldest days in Washington, D.C.'s history. Government offices shut down and workers went home. The snow turned to ice. No one was on the streets or in the Capitol quadrangle. We spent the nights just several blocks away from the White House, at the Center for Creative Non-Violence, America's largest shelter, headed by an old friend, Carol Fennelly. The shelter was filled to capacity, but Carol saved us some space on the floor.

We were a strange-looking group huddled under those blankets, steam coming out of our nostrils and ice forming at the tips of our mustaches and beards. We included lawyers, corporate executives, actors, film producers, war veterans, writers, social activists, architects, street people, Buddhists, Christians, Jews,

Muslims, men, women, Africans, and Americans. Each of us came from a different background, each of us had a different life story. But we all pondered the same question.

By the time I was fifty-five I'd been a Zen Buddhist priest for twenty-four years and a Zen teacher for eighteen. Before that I'd been an aerospace engineer with McDonnell-Douglas. I'd spent the last twelve years developing the Greyston Mandala, a group of for-profit and not-for-profit organizations based in Yonkers, New York, that revitalize inner-city neighborhoods by making low-cost housing, jobs, child care, and other supportive services available to Yonkers families. I felt that our community development projects were the deepest expressions of my Buddhist practice and teachings. Our latest project was the beginning of a housing and medical complex for people with HIV infection or AIDS.

As I approached my fifty-fifth birthday I felt something more was called for, but I wasn't sure what it was. I thought about the many wonderful social activists I'd met over the years who dedicated their lives to ending poverty, hunger, war, disease, racism, and violence in their communities and around the world. Many of them felt isolated and alone, with little support for their work. I also thought of the many more people I'd met, men and women, young and old, Buddhists and non-Buddhists alike, who had told me how much they wanted to change their world but that they didn't know where to start. They were discouraged and disempowered, feeling that nothing they could do would make a difference.

Each of my students and associates who joined me in Washington brought his or her perspective and life experience into our question. Together we pondered that question for five icy days. And when my birthday party ended, I had my answer.

I was going to found the Zen Peacemaker Order.

It would be a community of social activists and peacemakers from around the world. It would provide them with a home, a place where they could come together, tell their stories, and gather strength and new ideas before going back to their own communities and peace endeavors.

It would also be a place where they could explore the spiritual practice of peacemaking. This was very important to me. For years people had referred to me as a social service entrepreneur who developed new structures and organizations to meet the needs of the inner city. But I was a Zen Buddhist teacher as well. Zen is a practice that pushes us to experience, to realize and actualize, what is. As a Zen teacher, I was always asking myself what new practices I could develop to help my students experience the oneness of life. I was always addressing certain questions, such as: What keeps us feeling separate from each other? What keeps us thinking that we know the right way? What keeps us from seeing our unity, from appreciating everything as it is? And what are the peacemaking forms that will help all beings experience their interdependence?

At the Zen Peacemaker Order we would explore these questions and develop peacemaking practices to help us and all our brothers and sisters, from all cultures and traditions, experience the deep intimacy of no-separation, of the oneness that is our very own life.

The order would also be a training ground and a launching pad for the many people who said they wanted to do something but didn't know what. Here they would get training, inspiration, and opportunities to work with other peacemakers. They would find inside themselves the answers to their own questions. They would find out what peacemaking was about.

And what is peacemaking?

You won't find the answer in this book. This is not a book of answers, for there is little energy in answers. This is a book of questions. More precisely, it's about living a questioning life, a life of unknowing. If we're ready to live such a life, without fixed ideas or answers, then we are ready to bear witness to every situation, no matter how difficult, offensive, or painful it is. Out of that process of bearing witness the right action of making peace, of healing, arises.

This book describes that process. Members of the Peacemaker Order—from activists developing community in the inner cities of the Bronx and Yonkers to a prison inmate building a network of prison hospices across the country, from a teacher working with the dying to a war veteran exploring the meaning of peace and reconciliation in Vietnam—bear witness. Working and training with the order, they live an open, questioning life, plunging into certain situations with the faith that out of this process a spontaneous act of healing will arise.

So please don't read this book as if you have the questions and I have the answers. Read it as if we were talking to each other. I can't tell you how to make peace. But what I can tell you is how to give up our certainties and live life fearlessly; or, as we say in the order, how to penetrate the unknown, bear witness, and heal ourselves and all creations.

PART I

BEARING WITNESS
AT
AUSCHWITZ-BIRKENAU

A guard tower at Birkenau, 1996.

Retreat at Auschwitz

On the week of Thanksgiving 1996, on a cold, bright Sunday afternoon, a group of 150 people from around the world made its way to the town of Oświęcim in Poland. I went with them.

Oświęcim is an hour's drive directly east of the beautiful city of Kraków. It's a small industrial hub for railroad lines that crisscross the different regions of Poland, then plunge east to Russia, south to Slovakia and Hungary, and west to Germany and the rest of Europe. It was primarily this characteristic that in 1940 led the Nazis to build a large complex of death camps adjacent to Oświęcim, within walking distance from the center of town. That complex became known as Auschwitz-Birkenau, and the railway lines that converged on the town eventually brought more than one and a half million people to their deaths.

Earlier that Sunday morning we had a guided tour of Kazimierz, the old Jewish quarter of Kraków shown in Steven Spielberg's film *Schindler's List*. We wandered around a neighborhood that hadn't substantively changed in close to a century. More than seventy thousand Jews had once lived in Kazimierz. Old photographs show the central square on Szeroka Street, fronted by the old and graceful Remu Synagogue, filled with Polish Jews buying and selling goods in a flea market. But in 1996 the big square was practically empty. The narrow alleys were still there, the dim courtyards, the cemeteries and ruins, but they were empty. In 1996 there were almost no Jews in Kraków. It was estimated that there were at most five thousand Jews in all of Poland; in 1939 there had been more than two million.

For the rest of that week we were going to bear witness at Auschwitz-Birkenau. I wanted the retreat to start at Kazimierz so that people could see the life that once existed before going to the camps. After the great success of Spielberg's film, funds had begun to come in from abroad to rehabilitate Kazimierz, and as this was my third visit, I could see the difference those contributions had made. A few synagogues were being rebuilt, though it was not clear who would pray in them. Houses around the square had been renovated and newly painted. Restaurants featuring Jewish East European food had opened and there was even a Klezmer concert one evening. One could say that Kazimierz was becoming gentrified. We were told by our Polish hosts that it was on its way to becoming the Greenwich Village of Kraków.

After lunch we boarded the buses that brought us down to Oświęcim. Oświęcim is the town's Polish name. The Germans called it Auschwitz. The many Jews who lived there before the war called their town Oshpitzin, using the Yiddish word for *guests*. The residents of Oshpitzin, till their deaths, were renowned for their hospitality.

Our group included contingents from Poland,

Germany, the United States, Israel, Ireland, Italy, France, Holland, Switzerland, the Czech Republic, and Belgium. Among us were rabbis; Catholic nuns and monks; Buddhist priests, nuns, and teachers; a Sufi imam; and lay people from all walks of life. We would spend five full days at the camps. We would spend most of the daylight hours at Birkenau. Our accommodations were on-site, too: most of us in housing at the Auschwitz Museum, located in the camp known as Auschwitz 1, and others at an interfaith center a fifteen-minute walk away.

I was born to a Jewish family in Brooklyn. In December 1994 I'd visited Auschwitz for the first time on my own, and then had vowed to return two years later to lead a bearing witness retreat at the camps. Not a retreat just for Buddhists, Jews, or Christians, but for everyone—for people from different countries, backgrounds, and ethnic origins speaking different languages, people with different memories.

Hitler and Nazi Germany had been determined to stamp out differences. They had deified one race and one culture, declared all others inferior, and selected some to be exterminated. I was determined to bring people from different religions and nationalities to the very place where diversity had once been condemned to a terrible grave. There we would bear witness to our differences.

Out of that, a healing would arise. How this would happen or what shape the healing would take, I had no idea. But I was so sure it would happen that, in developing the retreat schedule, I decided to end the retreat with a Thanksgiving dinner. I felt certain that by the end deep appreciation and gratitude would arise and that we would wish to celebrate them in some way. But when people asked me how that would happen, I told them honestly that I didn't know.

— 2 —

Diversity at Auschwitz

The differences among us began to emerge while we were still on the buses, before we even got to the camps. I sat with my wife and children and looked around me. Some of the retreat participants I knew, others I didn't. Some were excited at being in a strange country, as if they were tourists. Others were happy to see old friends they hadn't seen for a long time. Some made conversation, some laughed. Others were pale and tense, their faces plastered to the windows, dread in their hearts. Some had had nightmares about this trip for weeks, including one woman who had visited a therapist in preparation for the retreat. Mostly they sat alone and looked out the windows at the black beech trees of the Polish countryside. Many were thinking about the Jewish folktales they'd heard and read, so many of which took place in such a landscape.

We had everyone here: survivors, children of survivors, children of Nazis, children of German soldiers, and children of refugees. We also had many people with no direct family connection to Auschwitz.

Though outside the trees were already bare, the grass was still green instead of being blanketed with snow. The fall of 1996 had been Poland's warmest fall on record.

The sign where the buses rolled in in mid-afternoon read AUSCHWITZ MUSEUM. One of my students told me she hated the word *museum*. "Why?" I asked her. "Because we Jews are the exhibit," she said.

Once at Auschwitz, most of the Jewish and German participants looked grimly around them, obviously ill-at-ease. Other Europeans were also restrained. Many Americans, on the other hand, smiled and chatted, as if this were a social occasion. And then there were our hosts, a contingent of some thirty Polish men and women, guarded and taciturn. They spoke a language few others understood. They looked awkward, as if they weren't sure what they were doing here. Many were Zen Buddhists who had come for the retreat because I was a Zen teacher. They obviously wished I'd chosen to lead a traditional Zen retreat with many hours of silent meditation in a secluded center in the countryside. Not a bearing witness retreat at Auschwitz.

There was tension even during our first meeting of facilitators and clergy. All those present were highly experienced clergy members, teachers, and therapists. But the meeting was quiet and subdued. I outlined our plans and reviewed the daily schedules. Midway through the meeting I received a note. A participant from Israel wished to talk to me urgently as soon as the meeting was over.

We sat down face-to-face. She was a Jewish woman who spent half her time in America and the other half in Israel. "I have to leave here," she told me. She didn't mean to be disrespectful, she didn't mean to criticize what we were doing, it was not up to her to pass judgment. She appreciated that we'd given her a scholarship for the retreat. But she couldn't stay. People had smiles on their faces. They were laughing in the hallways. They didn't understand where they were, they didn't understand how it felt for her to come here. Her heart was full of horror. Auschwitz was impossible. People's behavior was an affront.

I agreed with her. Auschwitz was impossible. It was all impossible. And still we had to do something. People had to come here. They had to bear witness.

She was uncertain. She took out her journal and read out loud, "What is the virtue of remaining hidden?" This was not a rhetorical question, she explained. There is no language for Auschwitz, no words. There are many who shun Auschwitz and say no one should ever go back there, it should be left to the dead. The words, the cries, the forms haven't been invented to deal with Auschwitz.

And still we have to do something, I told her. And I agreed with her: It was impossible.

I told her that this wasn't only one retreat but 150 separate retreats. Each person was doing his or her own thing, each person was dealing with it in his or her way. At any one moment someone was going to offend somebody else. Because the whole thing was impossible.

I asked her to think it over and told her that, if she still felt the same way, she could leave the next morning. She agreed. The following morning she still felt ill at ease. I could see her trailing behind the large group, privately immersed in her grief and sorrow. But she decided to delay her departure one more day. Then other participants began to talk to her. They shared with her how they were feeling and asked her for help and support. She began to engage with the very people who had previously offended her, the people who had looked at Auschwitz differently from her. She finally left one day before the end of the retreat, grateful for the opportunity to have been at Auschwitz with all of us.

She wasn't the only one who felt hurt and offended during that first day. Though I had spent a long, long time planning this retreat, it seemed as if every detail of that first day was guaranteed to upset somebody. Some thought it was a travesty that we were staying at the Auschwitz Museum. The rooms were on the second floor, over the museum, right on the grounds of Auschwitz 1, one of the three concentration camps that form the Auschwitz-Birkenau complex. If that wasn't bad enough, a small group was staying inside the camp itself, on the other side of the black gate that says *ARBEIT MACHT FREI,* inside the building that formerly housed SS officers and that is usually reserved for the use of historians and researchers. In the evening the grounds of the camp itself were locked up, but it was easy to get inside. At night, after our evening schedule ended, people would walk inside the camp along old barracks and cell blocks. They would walk in couples, speaking softly, or else alone. One night someone blew a shofar, a ram's horn used by Jews during prayer services on the Day of Atonement, at the site known as Execution Wall, where prisoners had been shot. The eerie wail was heard throughout the camp. Many were offended by this, too.

Some grieved, some talked. Some smiled and chatted, others were dumb with shock. This was how the retreat began. We'd come from different homes, religions, countries, and legacies to be together at Auschwitz. Everyone knew we were standing on hallowed ground. That meant there was powerful energy here, the energy of transformation. But it was up to us to hold it and work with it.

I could feel the discomfort, nervousness, and upset. And we were going to be together, in close quarters, for five days.

— 3 —

The Unknown at Auschwitz

In the morning we gathered to see a brief film on what the Russians had found when they liberated Auschwitz in 1945. After that we broke into four large groups for guided tours of the camps in English, Polish, German, and French.

I knew that the retreat participants would be overwhelmed by what they were going to see that day. But I didn't know how early this would happen or that it would start with my wife, Jishu. A Zen priest and teacher, Jishu had come down to Auschwitz on the buses with everyone else, but that first night she was unable to sleep. She could feel the restless spirits in the camp, the souls without repose. So she had sat up in her bed all night doing meditation practices of loving kindness for the benefit of these spirits. By the time morning came she was worn out. When she saw the documentary in the morning, with its photos of starving children and the pits full of corpses, she began to sob uncontrollably, and when the film ended she fainted. A doctor taking part in the retreat examined her and ordered her to go to bed and get some rest. So while the others went on their tour I remained with her in our room upstairs.

I didn't need to take the tour of the Auschwitz

Museum because I'd done it back in 1994 and seen the exhibits that the others were seeing now. So while Jishu rested I sat and thought back to that first visit. What had brought me to Auschwitz back then? What had I seen and experienced there? And what had moved me so much that I had vowed to return in two years' time and lead a retreat to bear witness at the death camps?

That first trip had taken place in the early days of December. I'd gone down to Oświęcim to participate in an international convocation, but my real reason for going was to meet with Claude Thomas.

Claude was a veteran of the Vietnam War. In a year-long tour of service as a helicopter gunner, beginning when he was only seventeen, Claude had killed several hundred Vietnamese. He was shot down and injured on many occasions; finally he was wounded so severely that it had cut short his military service, and he returned stateside. After years of drug and alcohol dependency, instability, homelessness, and violence, Claude began to work for peace. His work took him around the world, bringing a message of peace not just to war veterans but to all people who lead lives of conflict and violence. In 1994, Claude had joined a walk that was beginning at Auschwitz in Poland, continuing south through the war-torn Balkans, east across the Mediterranean to the Middle East, then down to India and Pakistan, across Southeast Asia to Vietnam, and culminating in Hiroshima on the fiftieth anniversary of the American bombing of that city.

In 1994, I had come to Poland to give Claude his first vows as a peacemaker at Auschwitz, at the beginning of his long walk. The following year he would be ordained.

That December had been a cold one in Poland, with the countryside covered with frost. A large interfaith group had gathered at the concentration camp complex. On that first day we'd visited the museum at Auschwitz 1 and seen its exhibits. Grisly evidence of dehumanization had confronted us everywhere: mountains of gray hair shorn from women about to be killed, huge collections of shaving brushes, luggage, clothes, and prosthetic devices. There were rooms full of baby and children's clothes. The endless rows of photos of gaunt, starved faces had stretched across wall after wall, faces staring at us out of hollow black eyes, the eyes of men and women who knew they were dying. We'd looked at their tattooed arms and striped uniforms. They had died there nameless and alone, forgotten by the world, dehumanized by their executioners. And still we were looking at only a tiny fraction of the dead of Auschwitz, for most of those murdered there, from every country in Europe as well as Russia, had been exterminated without a trace.

Everyone who visits Auschwitz sees these exhibits. Our groups were seeing them now, too. Though most had heard of the exhibits, seeing them was a very different thing. How would they react?

With my wife fast asleep, I left our room and walked inside the camp to the place known as Execution Wall. We had arranged for all of us to gather there after the Auschwitz tour. The tour usually ends with Block 11, right by Execution Wall, where prisoners condemned to be shot were imprisoned for the last days, sometimes hours, of their lives. At Block 11 visitors pass rooms where mock trials had been held and summary sentences quickly passed. In the basement they see the cells where the prisoners were kept, some as small and low as dog kennels, so that there was no room to sit up or even lie down. All a prisoner could do was crouch down on all fours and keep his or her head bowed. The cells were well within earshot of the wall, so the prisoners could hear the shots ringing out one after the next, knowing their turns were coming soon. Visitors saw the scratches on the walls that prisoners had made with their fingernails, carving out names and signs of the cross. Some thirty thousand people had been shot at Execution Wall with a single bullet to the back of the neck. That's where we met for our first Kaddish service (a Kaddish is the Jewish memorial prayer for the dead).

I watched as each group came out to the courtyard of the famous brick wall, with its eternal candles and flowers. I looked at their pale faces. No one was smiling anymore, certainly no one was laughing. Some were crying; most were in shock. Almost all of their faces said the same thing: "Get me out of here. I've seen Auschwitz and now I want to leave." They wanted to do what almost all other groups visiting Auschwitz do: board the bus and go home.

Memorial candles were given out and the Kaddish was said. Some people said the words, others did not. They seemed numb. For seeing Auschwitz for the first time is like a blow to the head. It leaves people's minds blank. Nothing they'd ever heard, seen, or read had prepared them for this. Like Jishu, they were on overload, they were in shock. Their usual concepts and ideas failed them, they didn't know what to think. They'd lost control.

They were in a space of unknowing. And now they were going to Birkenau.

Peacemaker Vows
at Auschwitz

We entered Birkenau in the afternoon. We walked through the gatehouse with the large masonry arched opening through which freight trains with human cargo had once arrived at Birkenau, its guard tower overlooking the camp.

As soon as we entered everyone looked around, stunned to silence by the camp's vastness, its interminable rows of barracks and the rectangles of rubble where barracks had once existed, and the long, seemingly endless railway track that stretched from the gate to the terminus, the extermination compounds. Barbed wire was strung out in long straight lines, broken only by guard towers and warnings in German that the wire was electrified.

Once again, as the groups followed their guides into the large complex of barracks and then, finally, down those terrible railroad tracks, I thought back to 1994, when I'd walked down those same tracks with Claude Thomas. We had entered Birkenau on the second day of our stay there, and immediately I had known that here, at Birkenau, I would do the ceremony giving him his peacemaker vows.

Then, as now, Birkenau's rows of barracks had gone as far as the eye could see, disappearing into the beautiful birches that stood at the camp's perimeter and lent it their name. It had been very cold and very damp, and while I shivered in my thick navy parka I'd thought of the inmates who had spent winter months here clad only in striped cotton uniforms.

We had walked down the train tracks, those same tracks that had represented literally the end of the line for a million and a half people who'd spent weeks in cattle cars before arriving here, their final destination. The tracks went on and on, flagged by guard towers and the blocks of barracks on either side, extermination sites marking both sides of its far end.

Bombed by the Nazis before they'd evacuated the camp, these killing sites form huge rectangles in the ground, the walls of the crumbled crematoria now large slabs of rock collapsed against one another. One still can't mistake where men, women, and children had descended down the steps into dressing areas where they'd been forced to strip in the freezing cold, then make their way to the adjoining gas chamber. The crematoria where their bodies were burned were connected via a series of flues to a single chimney that blazed day and night, belching the smell and ash of burning flesh. We gazed down at the small rooms where gold teeth had been extracted, where personal papers had been burned and all traces of life removed. And as I stood overlooking one of these extermination complexes, a vast industry of death, I suddenly knew that this was where I would give Claude Thomas his vows as a peacemaker. Here, on the steps of the crematoria, he would take refuge.

When the larger group left Birkenau, he and I settled down on the steps leading to the large crematoria walls that, in collapsing against each other, had formed a triangle. I sat on a blanket on the frozen ground and lit a memorial candle. Claude knelt in front of me. A small group of his friends stood around us. Some were veterans like him. The cold was extreme.

I began by thanking the souls that were there for giving us that space for the ceremony. As I said that, it began to rain. Cold raindrops fell on my shaved head, on Claude's long blond ponytail, on his red, folded hands. As part of the ceremony I gave Claude two new names: *Anshin* (meaning *heart of peace*) and *Angyo* (meaning *Peacemaker*). I wrote those names on the back of a small peacemaker robe that Claude subsequently wore over his chest every day of his walk for the next six months. I put my stamp and the date and place on the back of it: "December 6, 1994, Birkenau."

Claude then took sixteen peacemaker vows, each of which captures the essence of the peacemaker:

> I vow to be oneness.
> I vow to be diversity
> I vow to be harmony.
> I vow to penetrate the unknown.
> I vow to bear witness.
> I vow to heal myself and others.
> I vow not to kill.
> I vow not to steal.
> I vow not to be greedy.
> I vow not to tell lies.
> I vow not to be ignorant.
> I vow not to talk about others' errors and faults.
> I vow not to elevate myself by blaming others.
> I vow not to be stingy.

I vow not to be angry.

I vow not to speak ill of myself and others.

Each time I asked him, "Will you keep these vows?"

Each time Claude responded, "I will."

At the end of the ceremony we embraced. As our small group left the site of the crematorium a car drove down from the gate, a guard came out, passed us, and locked the gate behind us.

And even as we walked back along the railroad tracks that cold December day in 1994 to rejoin the large group waiting outside, I vowed that I would return to Auschwitz. I knew then that Auschwitz, for all its horrors, had a healing energy. I didn't know how or why, only that it had torn away everything I knew and pushed me into the unknown. I made a vow to return there in two years, during the week of Thanksgiving 1996, and lead a retreat. I even knew what we would do. We would sit on those same steps where I'd given Claude his new name of peace, at the same selection site, around those same tracks, and bear witness.

During the week of Thanksgiving 1996 I fulfilled my vow. We came back, 150 people strong, to be face-to-face with both the horror—and the healing—of Auschwitz.

— 5 —

The Souls of Auschwitz

This is the schedule we followed for the next four days:

The mornings began with meetings of small groups with facilitators. People of similar nationality and language met to share their feelings and their stories. After breakfast we assembled each day as one to go to Birkenau.

We walked for two miles past small farmhouses and furrowed pastures white with frost under gray, heavy skies. From a distance we could see Birkenau. We picked up our sitting mats and cushions at the large gatehouse and walked slowly down the tracks.

As a Zen Buddhist teacher, one of the practices that I had done and taught for many years was the practice of walking meditation. When you do that practice properly, regardless of whether you walk slowly or quickly, you become each step taken, each contraction and expansion of muscle, the ground beneath your feet, the heel that picks up and sets down. You take each step as if your life depends on it.

When you walk down the railroad tracks at Birkenau, you know that for more than a million people those steps down the tracks had indeed been their last. Row after row of prisoners had advanced to the selection site and had been "selected" by Dr. Mengele and his fellow SS doctors. Those healthy enough to work had been sent to the slave labor camp, which in most cases meant slow death from starvation, exposure, hard labor, and disease. The infirm, the elderly, mothers, and children went directly to the gas chambers. In the latter part of the war, when the Nazis were well aware that the war was lost, selections didn't even take place. Entire trainloads of people were marched down the tracks, step after step, to the extermination sites at the end.

We, too, walked down the tracks, and when we reached the selection site we put down our cushions and formed a large ellipse around the tracks.

Each period of meditation began and ended with the blowing of the shofar. Its full, wailing tones seemed to penetrate everywhere, reaching not just the people who sat in that great circle but also into the decomposing barracks and the large death chambers. We were dressed warmly, but as the hours went by the cold crept inside, chilling us to the bone. It was impossible not to think of prisoners shivering in striped cotton uniforms, dying of the cold in barracks close to where we sat. The skies were almost always gray, but the gray changed from day to day. Twice there was snow. Both times it was a gentle snow that slowly covered our mats and cushions, then our coats, hats, and mufflers. No one stirred.

But we weren't silent. During the meditation we chanted the names of the dead. Three people sat at each of four points of the ellipse. The first of the three chanted for ten minutes the names of individuals who'd died in Auschwitz. Then the second person took over, then the third. The four voices, one at each point, carried across the large, silent circle. The names were taken from the Death Books compiled by the Gestapo, but they also included names sent to us by retreat participants of relatives who had died at Auschwitz and in other holocausts. The names in the Death Books had been listed in alphabetical order, so sometimes the chanter read the same family name over and over again, wondering how many had come from the same family. They chanted the names carefully, laboring lovingly and attentively over their long, sometimes strange-sounding syllables.

HILDEGARD EGNER-REINHARDT,
4.9.1932–13.3.1944
SAMUEL EHENTREU, 15.8.1907–11.5.1942
ADALBERT EHRENFELD, 2.6.1890–4.5.1942

We didn't chant their dates of birth and death, or the cities where they had come from, though sometimes these were listed, too. But the dates were a reminder that the old, the middle-aged, and the very, very young had all been put to death right where we sat.

AUGUSTE ELSTER, 27.3.1875–23.3.1944
KONSTANT ELSTER, 23.8.1941–20.4.1944
MERANIE ELSTER, 19.10.1943–17.2.1944
SIEGFRIED ERICHON, 3.11.1910–5.5.1942

When they finished chanting the names, the four readers would walk to the middle of the circle. There they would put the lists of the dead in a red lacquered box that lay on the cold, slippery rocks. During the days other things appeared around the box: candles, incense sticks, mezzuzahs, beads, single roses, and even a Hawaiian lei.

The shofar blew again. It took a while for us to get to our feet, stiff and numb from the cold. Then, slowly and mindfully, we walked together to the extermination sites at the end of the tracks. My friend and student Don Singer, a rabbi and Zen teacher, would pause in front of the gate to the killing site and lead us in singing: "*Pitchu li sha-arey tsedek. Avo vam hode-Ya.* [Open the gates of righteousness. I will enter and thank Thee]." Then, overlooking death chambers, crematoria, and ash pits, we would say the Kaddish.

Traditionally, the Kaddish is said by mourners during the year following the passing of a loved one. The prayer extols God even in the worst of times, in the middle of the most terrible suffering and loss: "Throughout all space, bless, bless this great name, throughout all time." As the retreat progressed, other groups of participants who didn't speak English also wished to say the Kaddish, so with Don's help they translated it into their respective languages. Soon we began to say the prayer in different languages, first in the original combination of Hebrew and Aramaic, then in English, then in French, Polish, German, and finally Italian.

We walked back out of Birkenau in the middle of the day for soup and bread (no food is permitted inside the camp). The soup was given out in plastic bowls. We had to keep our bowls with us and bring them to and from Birkenau every day. We asked participants not to use spoons. After lunch we went back inside the camp and returned to our circle around the railroad tracks.

We also had services. As soon as we arrived in Birkenau in the morning we would break into four religious groups: Jewish, Buddhist, Christian, and Moslem. Each group then walked to a site it chose for prayers. Some went to the extermination compounds, some to the end of the tracks where plaques and simple stone monuments in many languages commemorate the dead, and some to the barracks. We could hear the melodies of their prayers: the Jewish Kaddish, the Christian Misericordias Domini, the Buddhist Gate of Sweet Nectar, and readings from the Islamic Koran. We stayed at Birkenau all day and closed with an interfaith service. Leaders of the four religious traditions gathered, lit one candle together, and then led the entire group in prayer. After that we all picked up our cushions and mats and began the long walk back to the gatehouse.

We spent four full days at Birkenau in this way, from the morning hours to twilight. On that first day after the tour of the museum and our first walk into Birkenau, people had moved slowly and reluctantly, as if in a dream. "It's too much for one day," one teacher told me before we walked down the tracks. "Let's go back and begin again tomorrow."

But I wanted us to start to bear witness that very afternoon. People were in a state of shock and despair. I had seen it with Jishu the previous night and early that morning, and now it was on everyone's faces. I thought of the many people who had told me they weren't coming to Auschwitz in order to avoid such powerful feelings. I thought of the many more I'd known throughout my teaching years for whom losing control was to be avoided at all costs.

And yet, it was precisely now, with our usual defenses and protective mechanisms gone, that we could begin to bear witness. Auschwitz had stripped us bare, just as it had done to me two years before, thus creating a special space for us, a space of bearing witness. We sat in our circle for four days, listening to the names of the dead. And as the days passed our circle became bigger. We made more room for ourselves and the pain we carried inside. We made more room for the people sitting next to us. And finally, we made more and more room for the dead whose names were being chanted moment after moment. With each passing day, our circle grew and grew.

What I remember best is the last sitting of each day, at twilight. It was late and other visitors would be gone. The sun would set and the names of the dead would be chanted. The twilight and the names would hover over us, over the barracks, the extermination compounds, the railroad tracks, over all of Birkenau. Motionless, we would sit and listen. Once it rained, so lightly and gently that it felt like tears. We'd sit and listen, feeling the souls of Auschwitz all around us.

For there were souls here.

In preparing for the retreat I had contacted my old friend Rabbi Zalman Schachter-Shalomi and asked for his advice. Reb Zalman had said that it was important to remember why we were doing this. We were not doing this for ourselves, he said, or for the sake of our experience or understanding, not even for our own grief. We were doing this for the souls left at

Auschwitz, cut off from life quickly and abruptly, unable to find rest. Our retreat was for the sake of those souls, to help bring them to rest.

In Zen practice we say that we do our sitting meditation not for ourselves but for the world. At Auschwitz we sat around the tracks for the living and also for the dead. Wherever we were—seated around the railroad tracks, penetrating the gloom inside the barracks, looking down at the ruins of death chambers, examining the ruins that extended as far as the eye could see—we were accompanied by the souls of Auschwitz.

— 6 —

Healing at Auschwitz

In the evenings we gathered as one group. Interpreters translated what was being said into several different languages. Many people wore headphones.

The first evening was hard. No one wished to tell stories.

I had seen this reluctance two years before, on my first visit to Auschwitz. What I particularly remember was an encounter between the American-born son of a Jewish concentration camp inmate and the German daughter of the Nazi commandant of that same camp. For many years the American had heard stories from his father about the brutality of the camp commandant, and coming face-to-face with the man's daughter in Auschwitz had been almost intolerable for him. He didn't want to meet or talk to her, he wanted to remain silent. But when the two finally talked and exchanged stories, they had discovered they had many things in common, including shame, guilt, and silence. The expected anger of that first meeting had eventually evolved into a deep and powerful bond of understanding and empathy, and finally into a strong, meaningful friendship.

Now, too, some participants began to tell their stories. But it was never easy.

A Dutch woman had been a child of three when her parents were taken by the Nazis, never to return. She had been saved by friends and was later told that because she had been a happy, noisy child her parents had decided it was too risky to go into hiding with her.

The American daughter of a Jewish survivor of Auschwitz discovered later in life that she had a German half brother, the son of her father and a German woman he'd met after the war.

The daughter of a Nazi talked about the silence in which she had grown up. Her family lived in America, and though the past seemed far behind them, the silence was always there.

The daughter of a survivor talked of the bedtime stories she'd been told as a child—not children's stories or Dr. Seuss, but stories of fear and hiding, of torture and killing.

The daughter of a German soldier told of discovering her father's war letters to her mother from the Russian front, letters idealizing Adolf Hitler and Nazism, vowing to win the battle for his Führer.

A German man talked of his uncle, who'd never had children—he had been sterilized for not joining the SS, to the enormous shame of his entire family.

Sometimes people stopped and couldn't go on. They needed help. Rabbi Singer led everyone in singing Jewish melodies. He reminded them that a whole heart is a broken heart. Once he even led them in dance.

Listening to the people speak, I was struck by the fact that though their families had come from different sides of the conflict and their stories seemed so different, what many had in common was the secrecy surrounding the past. What they remembered most was the silence in their families about the war, about disappeared relatives and mysterious photographs. This was often accompanied by depression. In all cases the discovery of the truth about their parents and their families, and their coming to terms with their heritage, was a turning point in their lives. It not only put their family past into perspective, it also radically affected their relationships with themselves, their spouses, and their children.

As the evenings passed, more and more people wanted to talk. It turned out that a group of people staying in the former SS barracks was gay. One evening a gay man declared with pride in his voice that in the rooms where SS officers had once lived homosexuals now gathered to cut pink triangles.

A French journalist spoke. She was a mother. As she sat in our circle in Birkenau, she said, all she could think about was what it was like for a mother to come down the steps with her children, hounded by guards and dogs, take their clothes off, and lead them, naked, to the gas chamber. She couldn't get it out of her mind.

Soon it was obvious to everyone that something was happening. We were growing intimate with each other, and intimate with Auschwitz. Our differences didn't disappear. The horror of the death camp didn't go away for one minute. We were becoming a family, a very large family that included not just us but all the inhabitants of Auschwitz.

I think it began with the reading of the names of the dead. At first some people didn't want to do this, saying they preferred to sit in silence. And then, suddenly, people urgently asked for a turn to read names. And after they'd had their turn they wanted another turn, and another, again and again. A young German man with poor vision begged the staff to find some way to magnify his list so that he'd be able to chant the names, too. The red lacquered box on the tracks in the middle of the circle became a magnet. People went back to it again and again, putting some names away and taking out new names for chanting.

For these weren't just names. They were the dead come to life, each name a different story, each name a whole, though interrupted, life. The dry bones burned to ashes and buried in the ash pits became alive. Not just the dry bones of the Auschwitz dead, but the dry bones of our own lives, the parts we feared and hated, the parts we'd run away from.

As people chanted the names I'd hear them pause. Later they'd tell me that they'd chanted a familiar name, similar to the name of someone they knew, sometimes even a name exactly like their own. For in chanting the names of the dead, we were chanting our own names, too. The dry bones were none other than our own, long rejected by us, and now, at Auschwitz, come to life.

Sometimes it was hard for people to stay in the circle, so they would leave and walk around the camp. They would study the maps at the gatehouse to see where prisoners of different nationalities had been kept and then they'd go to visit the barracks of the women, the barracks of the Gypsies, the barracks of the families from the Terezin concentration camp, the barracks of the Russian or the Polish soldiers, the barracks of the children. They'd disappear inside the doorways and stroke the old, decaying wood of the bunks where three people had once slept side by side. In the evenings they'd share with us what they had seen: deer tracks on the paths between the birches, ruins in the shape of a man's face, a falcon overhead, a dove.

As our relationship with Auschwitz changed, so did the relationships among ourselves. Even our Polish hosts began to open up. At first they'd felt bewildered and resistant, numbed by what had happened to their country. Millions of Poles had died during the war. Warsaw had been leveled. The Germans were followed by the Russians. The Poles had suffered greatly. Auschwitz was just another monument to their seemingly endless suffering.

Finally the evening came when they, too, began to talk. Some were Jews who'd discovered their Jewish identity only recently, well into their adulthood. Some told of abusive fathers, former soldiers who wouldn't talk about the war, who drank in order to forget. Almost all came from families with secrets. A Polish actress spoke about the stolid silence of the Polish people in the face of so much suffering. "Enough silence!" she urged her countrymen. It was time to speak.

And people spoke. They struggled to articulate something they'd never believed possible, certainly not on the day when they'd first seen the camp. Birkenau was no longer "another planet," as someone had characterized it that first day. Men, women, and children had lived there. One hundred and sixty babies had been born at Auschwitz. So now our group walked carefully, even lovingly, over the frozen, slippery railroad tracks that once brought so many to their deaths. More than once I saw people stroking the rocks that lay among the ruins of the ovens and gas chambers. One Jewish woman stroked the barbed wire that stretches everywhere in the camps. Two of her aunts, an uncle, and a cousin had died at Auschwitz. The wire was as close as she would ever get to them, and she touched it gently.

And one evening a Frenchman finally spoke aloud the feeling that was in so many people's hearts. Michel Dubois' relatives had died at Auschwitz and coming here was a sad, painful reunion. But the more pain he felt, the more joy and love he felt, too. Love rises from the souls in this place, he declared. Love rises from Auschwitz and from Birkenau.

That love brought us all together. Our differences no longer divided us. Where previously there had been silence, anxiety, and even anger, we now had harmony, humor, and a deep appreciation of ourselves and of each other. We had become a family.

And in the mornings we returned to Birkenau. We always went back to the train tracks and the death chambers. We'd chant once more the names of the dead and bear witness again and again, deeper and deeper, to the anguish and suffering of that terrible place.

Once, after a meditation period, we stood by the ruins of a crematorium and recited the Kaddish. This time we recited it for the many children who'd died at Auschwitz. After we finished we waited for Don Singer to speak. Rabbi Singer was almost always warm and joyful. Day and night he'd remind us that joy and laughter existed everywhere, including in Auschwitz. He'd often say that one could not talk of God without talking of joy. But this time even Don was silent. This time even Don could not summon that joy. Instead he stared into the large extermination chambers, where so many babies had died, saying nothing.

And then from the back of the large group a woman began to sing. Don listened, then began to sing with her. We all joined in. And soon the German and Swiss participants sang German lullabies for the children who'd died at Auschwitz. A Swiss nun led them in singing.

There are many ways to express a broken heart: tears, laughter, silence, dance, and even German lullabies. You don't find wholeness till you're ready to be broken. Evening after evening we found new ways to express our brokenness. Each time we did this, a healing arose.

And in the mornings we always went back to Birkenau. It was an endless, continuous practice.

On the last day of our retreat we sat in Birkenau until late in the afternoon. During the last period of meditation we read aloud the names of the dead together. The air was filled with 150 voices calling out the names of people whose lives and deaths we'd grown to know intimately over the previous several days. The air was filled with our different voices, different accents, reciting the names of French people, Russians, Germans, Jews, Christians, Gypsies, homosexuals, Poles, Italians, Rumanians, Hungarians, and so many others who had died there. They were our names, too. Finally, as we approached the end, our voices died out and we finished in a long silence as, one by one, we returned our names to the red box in the middle of the tracks, surrounded by memorial candles. The sun set and we sat together in half darkness at Birkenau for the last time, and the candles continued to burn around the red lacquered box.

At the close of the day the shofar blew many times, following the pattern used to bring the Jewish Day of Atonement to a close every year. This time it brought our Auschwitz–Birkenau retreat to a close.

It was Thanksgiving Day 1996.

— 7 —

Oneness in Diversity

I have done many, many retreats over my life, and each time there is one particular lesson that I learn. What I learned from our retreat at Auschwitz-Birkenau was this: The thing we have in common is our diversity.

We all wish for more. We yearn to find things that are common to all human beings, around which we can come together. But underlying that yearning is the desire for people to be the same, to be the same as us, to affirm our way of seeing things. And that's the trap.

By the time our retreat ended at Auschwitz, it had become a one-people event. Adolf Hitler had also wanted a one-people event. His way of doing it was to eliminate diversity. He created hundreds of places like Auschwitz and Birkenau where he could destroy diversity and create one people who looked the same, thought the same, lived the same. But he couldn't do it. Because the one thing we ultimately have in common is that we're all different.

When we accept that everything is different we begin to see the oneness of life. Trying to find oneness without accepting those differences can take us on an endless quest that leads nowhere except to tremendous suffering for all beings.

Living with differences is not easy. Throughout our time together people came to me with advice on how to do things better: We shouldn't permit the Our Father prayer at Birkenau; we shouldn't have Islamic prayers at all; we shouldn't translate the Kaddish; we should do more meditation; we should do less; we should talk more; we should talk less. They had many ideas about what would make them feel more comfortable. But the retreat wasn't about making any of us comfortable. It was about bearing witness to our differences.

And during those five days we came together—not despite our differences, but because of them, because we acknowledged and honored them. Out of our diversity, we became one. By the time we came together for Thanksgiving dinner, this feeling was unmistakable.

All of this came out of a process of bearing witness: chanting the names of the dead, telling our stories, living with each other, living at Auschwitz for five full days, and taking it into our very marrow.

Bearing witness is not something to be done only at Auschwitz. When we bear witness to the unfolding of our daily lives, not shrinking from any situation that arises, we learn. We open to what is. And in that process, a healing arises.

The rest of this book is about bearing witness to the wholeness of life. It's about the teachings and the practices that are the foundation of the Zen Peacemaker Order and the people who embody some of those teachings. It will tell you how we actually formed the order in the summer of 1996—not out of ideas or preconceived notions, but out of the unknown.

PART II

BEARING WITNESS
TO THE
WHOLENESS OF LIFE

Bernie Glassman, Auschwitz, 1996.

— 8 —

Making Whole

If you were to ask me "What is the essence of Buddhism?" I would answer that it's to awaken. And the function of that awakening is learning how to serve.

In most mystical traditions, the role of the mystic—and of the peacemaker—is to make whole. Making peace is making whole. This is not just my definition but the definition of religious leaders and thinkers of many traditions. In fact, the word *peacemaker* in Hebrew is two words: *Oseh Shalom. Oseh: maker. Shalom: peace.* The Jewish mystics like to move around the vowels of a root word and see what emerges. If you do that to the root of *Shalom,* you get *Shalem,* which means *whole.* To make peace means to make whole.

The Jewish Kabbalists believed that in the beginning there was only the divine light, and that in creating the world God shattered it into an infinite number of sparks. That tradition emphasizes *Tikkun Olam,* the healing of the universe, restoring the fragments into the Whole.

A similar African folktale tells about Hilolombi, the Creator, who held a lamp in his hand that brought light into the world. But after his firstborn, Kwan, committed incest with his mother, Hilolombi dropped the lamp and it shattered into a thousand pieces. To bring the light back to the earth, human beings began to pick up these fragments, and today each person is in possession of one fragment, believing that he has the whole lamp. Unless we join together, the fullness of light will never return to the earth.

Making peace, making things whole, is an endless task. There are many definitions of a peacemaker. One of these I like most is that a peacemaker, knowing that the well needs water, climbs the mountain to reach the snow, gets a spoonful of snow, comes down, drops it in the well, and goes back up the mountain. She knows that the task is endless but she does as much of it as she can, day after day after day.

In my many years of teaching, numerous people have told me that making peace between fighting nations, building homes for the homeless, creating jobs for the unemployed, feeding hungry children in the world, and taking care of people with AIDS are overwhelming. And my answer always is, yes, it's overwhelming. That's why we never stop doing it.

In Buddhism we have different images and symbols. One of my favorites is Kannon, the image of compassion. Kannon can be a male or a female. There are different physical images of Kannon, but one shows Kannon with many, many arms. Why does Kannon have so many arms? I believe it is because when Kannon took the vow to make peace among all sentient beings she was so overwhelmed by the enormity of what that meant that she burst apart into millions of pieces. But the energy of that same vow brought all those pieces back in the shape of a million arms. Each arm holds something different. One arm holds a watch, one holds glasses, one arm bears a pen, one a hoe, one arm a Christmas bag, one a condom. Each arm has something different for the proper occasion.

Each of us is an arm of Kannon, enabling Kannon to do her work. Like her, we're also over-whelmed, but when we realize that the millions of pieces are all of us operating as one, then there's no problem. The reason we get overwhelmed is that we're attached to a certain result or that we want to achieve a certain goal. If we weren't attached we wouldn't be overwhelmed. It's endless. And we just take one step after the next.

At Auschwitz, Claude's step was to take peace-maker vows. In the years that followed, my wife, Jishu, and I also took our next step and cofounded the Zen Peacemaker Order. All members of the order take peacemaker vows. The order is also based on the Three Tenets: unknowing, or letting go of fixed ideas; bearing witness to joy and suffering; and healing ourselves and the universe. It was that first visit to Auschwitz in 1994 that helped me to appreciate the importance of the Three Tenets, not just for Zen Buddhists, not just for social activists, but for all people.

In the following chapters we will study these vows and tenets. First, let me say this. Peacemaker vows are not meant to separate us from other people. Their purpose is not to provide entree to a special club of peacemakers that is separate from other human beings. Even when we make certain tangible things for the cer-emony, such as a peacemaker robe or a necklace of beads representing the people who support our work, these are not status symbols. They are symbols of connection and harmony, not separation. Claude wore his short peacemaker robe over his chest day in and day out, in the freezing rain of the Balkans, under the hot May sun in Cambodia, and in the monsoons of Vietnam. It became like a second skin, stained and worn, full of the dust and sweat of many months' walking, connected with every place he went and everyone he met.

At Auschwitz I gave Claude a bracelet of beads as a gift to wear around his wrist on his walk. Buddhists, like Catholics, use beads as aids to their practice. In January, a month after he received the beads in Auschwitz, Claude's walk brought him to Bosnia. He and his group were often stopped by soldiers and prevented from traveling to certain destinations. Other members of that group were also peace activists walking through war-torn countries for peace, but when they saw soldiers they didn't want to talk to them. For them soldiers were bad. The guns they carried were bad. Many of these peace activists wanted to have nothing to do with the soldiers. Claude, on the other hand, sought them out.

One night he struck up a conversation with a Bosnian soldier. He asked him how he felt.

The soldier said he was fine.

Claude asked him how he was sleeping. Since the Vietnam War, Claude himself had gone sleepless most nights. He had insomnia, he had nightmares, he heard people screaming in his sleep. He was used to not sleeping.

The soldier understood then that Claude had once been a soldier himself. So he shook his head. He wasn't sleeping so well.

Then the two really started talking. The soldier explained what he was doing, Claude explained what he was doing. Then the soldier began to admire the beads that Claude wore around his wrist, the beads I'd given him at Auschwitz.

"I'll trade the beads for that gun," Claude told him, pointing to the nine-millimeter revolver in the soldier's hands.

The soldier said no. He wasn't allowed to let go of his gun. If he was caught without it he'd be shot.

So Claude said, "I'll trade the beads for the bullet in the chamber of that gun."

The soldier agreed, and they made the trade. Claude gave away the beads I'd given him, and in return he received the bullet from the chamber of the soldier's gun.

Whatever Claude received from me that cold afternoon at Auschwitz he used to connect, deeply and empathically, with another human being, a soldier. He didn't use his robe, his beads, or his vows to remain separate. Those beads connect that Moslem soldier to Claude Thomas, a Buddhist peacemaker, and to an entire order of peacemakers. Whether that soldier knew it or not, from that moment his life had changed.

Claude's life also changed. And for those of us who heard this story when he came back to the United States, our life changed, too, as yours has now that you have read it.

I like to tell the story of the Net of Indra, the ancient Indian king of the gods who wished to build a great monument to himself. He built a net that extended throughout all space and time, and each node of the net contained one bright and shining pearl. The net had an infinite number of pearls, with each pearl reflecting not just every other pearl but also the entire Net of Indra.

Claude's beads contain not just his life, not just the life of the Moslem soldier, but your life, my life, and every single life on this planet. The soldier's bullet also contains all of life. Our actions—whether they make peace or war—reverberate throughout this universe. Since we're all interdependent, nothing is small, trivial, or inconsequential. Not even a string of beads. Not even one bullet—or one word.

I Vow to Be Oneness

The first peacemaker vows taken by all members of our Peacemaker Order are:

> I vow to be oneness.
> I vow to be diversity.
> I vow to be harmony.

Many of the men and women who study with me come to spiritual practice from their intuitive grasp of life's interdependence, its oneness. In fact, they often have some experience of this unity before they begin to practice. Whether through a walk in the woods, an intimate conversation with another human being, or listening to a Beethoven symphony, we somehow intuit that we are all part of the same thing, part of a unity.

At the same time we know that this is not how we function most of the time. We human beings possess a number of characteristics that separate us from the experience of oneness. One is the brain. The brain operates dualistically, that's the way it thinks. When I'm aware of something, I'm aware of it as other, as other than myself. Whenever we're aware of other people, we're aware of them as separate from ourselves.

We don't always think dualistically. For instance,

I don't go around being aware of having a stomach—unless, of course, something is wrong with it. If I have a pain, if there is an illness in the stomach, I become aware of it. Whenever I go someplace I usually take myself along so I don't say "Bernie is here" when I arrive. If I say "Bernie is here," I'm aware of myself as separate from me. According to the norms of our society, that's considered mental illness.

In the same way, my awareness of other people and things already implies that they're separate from me. And that is our social illness, the illness of separation. If I truly experience myself as one, I don't announce "Bernie is here" when I arrive at the airport, I take it for granted. In the same way, if you truly experience the oneness of life and you come across a homeless man sitting on a New York City street, you won't ask the question Is that my brother? You'll take it for granted and take care of your brother. Because he's you.

But due to our dualistic brain, this is not how we usually function, and this is why many of us come to spiritual practice. As I said before, many mystical traditions are about bringing the pieces back into unity, making the fragments whole. They often have different names for that unity: the Infinite, the Absolute, the Divine, the One, God. Some of the most important words in Judaism are: "Listen O Israel, the Lord our God, the Lord is One."

These traditions not only teach us about unity, each of them has designed practices to help us experience it. Prayer and meditation are two such practices—but almost anything we do can become a practice to help us make the fragments whole.

What does it mean to make the fragments whole? Making whole means seeing that each piece is the whole. Everything as it is, is the whole. Mother Teresa said that everywhere she looked, she saw Christ. The sick, the dying, the poor, the maimed were all Christ. And she took care of Christ wherever she went.

Most of the time we have distinctions. We pick and choose. Some things are Christ and some aren't. Some things are divine, some things are not. Some things are the Way but not others. When we vow to be oneness, we vow to see everything as the Buddha, as Christ, as the Way. Because the Way is everything. It's not a particular direction or a special way of doing something, it's a circle with no outside and no inside, just the pulsating of life everywhere. It excludes nothing. Therefore, as peacemakers working in the world, we exclude nothing. We'll pick and choose according to what's appropriate for us at a certain place and a certain moment. But we won't be attached to what we choose, for everything is the Way.

For example, I have met many social activists who believe that everyone is the Way except rich people. They're comfortable going into shelters and food pantries, they mingle easily with people on the streets of our inner cities, but they can't say hello to someone with a lot of money. In their case it's not the poor and dispossessed who are the Other, it's the rich.

When peacemakers vow to be oneness, there is no Other.

I like to use the metaphor of my body. My right hand won't attack my left hand unless there's an illness that makes the right hand think it's separate from the left. If there's a gash in my left leg and blood is spurting out, my hands don't say, "Too bad, let the leg take care of itself, we're too busy to take care of it right now." They don't talk about how my body is all one, they just function that way. If my stomach is hungry my right hand doesn't say, "I'm too busy to put food in the mouth."

But that's what happens in life, in society. And it happens only because we have an illness called separation. If we don't see that the hands, legs, feet, head, and hair are all one body, we don't take care of them and we suffer. If we don't see the unity of life, we don't take care of life and we suffer.

Seeing the oneness of life doesn't mean that we accommodate every form of life. It doesn't mean an end to destruction. When cancer arises we have to do violent things so that the system may live. But the more I'm aware of the oneness of my body—including the cancer—the better I can take care of it. We all have cells that multiply, only in some cases they turn malignant and spread quickly. A healthy body is in a state of balance; malignant cells are quickly destroyed, while others are left alone. If I let the cancer spread unhindered, my body will go out of balance. But if I can see the wholeness of my body, including both malignant and nonmalignant cells, I will take care of the whole thing and restore balance to the system.

Seeing the oneness of life doesn't eliminate drastic measures. But by taking everything into account, we can choose the measures that will create the least harm to the system.

There's a Buddhist service in which we say, "I am the Buddhas and they are me." You are the Buddha,

I am the Buddha. I am you and you are me. When peacemakers take the vow to be oneness, we're vowing to see everything we encounter—every person, event, and phenomenon—as the Way, as Christ, as ourselves.

That means that everything and everybody must be taken care of.

— 10 —

I Vow to Be Diversity

If we could live in the world as if everything and everyone is Buddha, or Christ, or the divine, we would take care of each situation that arises in a natural and spontaneous way. But almost all of us exclude someone or something. It might be a person of a darker or lighter skin color, someone with a strong body odor because she lives on the streets and hasn't washed in several weeks, or someone coming at you with a knife. Or, as we saw during our time at Auschwitz, it could be someone from a different nationality or religion doing something we don't like. It happens moment after moment. Most of the time we're not even aware of it.

In his preface to his poignant account *Survival in Auschwitz,* Primo Levi wrote this: "Many people—many nations—can find themselves holding, more or less wittingly, that 'every stranger is an enemy.' "

When we see someone who doesn't look like us, who has different customs from ours, and who speaks a strange language, a slow process of dehumanization begins. We may not consciously think badly of him or even wish him harm, but we don't believe that he is quite as human as we are. This is often a subtle process, and noticing it requires attention, honesty, and sensitivity. Sometimes it's not subtle at all, and people begin to act out of these conceptions, denying others basic rights and freedoms. And when they do, Levi says, "then, at the end of the chain, there is the *Lager* [the concentration camp]." Auschwitz happened because human beings condemned to death others who were different from them. And though I had practiced the vow to be diversity for many years, that vow took on added significance for me after Auschwitz.

As we discovered at our retreat, it's very hard to accept differences. You might think that a group like ours, many of them peacemakers, many of them religious practitioners, would have had an easy time of it, but that is not the case. Sometimes the spiritual search after oneness becomes a search for sameness, and sometimes even a search for sameness with me.

I recently heard about a United Nations study that found that of some fifty-five wars currently being waged in the world today, two thirds are due to religious differences. What this often means is that two groups of people who believe in some form of unity are fighting each other. Both see that unity in their own image. What they don't see is the variety of life. They're comfortable with one thing, not many.

That's why we take the vow to be diversity. For diversity is the other side of oneness. It is the world of form in all its infinite variety of textures, colors, contrasts, and differences. Not only are we different from each other, but everything is different from one moment to the next—everything is change. We are all part of one single unity, but we're also very different. We can't do peacemaking in the world—in fact, we can't do anything effective in the world—without taking our differences into account.

Several years ago I met Bobbie Louise Hawkins, a writer who at that time was teaching in Boulder, Colorado. She asked her students to eavesdrop on conversations. These conversations could be taking place on the street, in an elevator, or in a store. Her students had to write the conversation down verbatim and then read it out loud. In her performances, Hawkins read conversations overheard at hotels, on the streets, even in insane asylums. People were amazed at the many voices they heard—not just the different thoughts or feelings being expressed but also the different nuances, words, and sounds. What they heard is the world of diversity.

It's very important to appreciate life in all its different manifestations, in all its manyness. People who focus too much on the oneness of life without seeing its diversity will sometimes establish a single standard for what is human. When we vow to be diversity we vow to work with all forms of life. We work with them by becoming them, by seeing their point of view and looking at life through their individual perspective. No matter who we work with, it's impossible to be an effective peacemaker without taking differences into account.

— II —

I Vow to Be Harmony

Vowing to be harmony, I accept that oneness and diversity are the same thing.

Does that sound like a contradiction? Yet that is exactly what happened during our Auschwitz retreat. In honoring our diversity, we discovered our oneness. By accepting our differences, we came together as one people.

In doing so we didn't lose our differences. Jews remained Jews, Buddhists remained Buddhists, Germans remained Germans, and so on. And yet, in the end, we were one people.

Once again, I'll use my body as an example. My body is just one body, yet it has many features. It has hands, toes, and thousands of hairs and pores (each different from the others). It has skin, bones, blood, guts, and various organs. It has many feet of intestines. But it's just one body—with millions of features and characteristics. Hurt one finger and the entire body feels it, everything's affected. If I eat food, what part is not affected? Breathe—what part is not affected?

We can look at it from the point of view of oneness and say it's one body, or we can look at it from the point of view of diversity and just see the features. They're two different ways of looking at the same thing.

In Auschwitz we were one group of people that came together to bear witness. Alternately, we were men, women, Buddhists, Jews, Christians, Moslems, agnostics, and many other distinctions and categories. Both refer to the same gathering; both are true. In the beginning we noticed only the distinctions. By the time the retreat ended, we experienced our oneness, too. In fact, we discovered that one is not possible without the other.

Peacemakers work with all of the features of the world, all of life's infinite varieties and phenomena. But we work with them out of intimacy and a sense of oneness, not out of separation. Out of this intimacy we take action.

For instance, if my hand is badly burned I immediately take care of it. I don't stand around saying "Look at that, what a terrible burn! Should I do something about it or shouldn't I?" I don't write books about how unfair it is, nor do I ignore it. It can't be ignored! The hand and I are not separate. When it gets burned, I take care of it. I do something.

The same is true with everything in life. I do something—not everything, that's impossible, but definitely something. If my child is in tremendous pain and suffering, I become that tremendous pain and suffering because there's no separation between my child and me. I don't ask questions like "How do I stop this?" or "Why is this happening?" I simply do the best I can to take care of my child.

Since I've taken the vow to be diversity, I'm ready to work with everything that comes up: children left homeless by an earthquake in Central America, an oil spill off the coast of Japan, grass that needs watering in my backyard, a little girl who fell off her tricycle and bruised her knee, a car that won't start on a cold morning, tree branches that need pruning. The list is endless. But whatever I do, I do out of oneness, not separation.

Harmony is the world of formless form. In vowing to be harmony, we vow to move freely in both the world of form and the world of oneness simultaneously, without getting stuck in one or the other.

The Jewish scholar and thinker Rabbi Abraham Isaac Kook said that the Circle of Life includes many groups of all kinds. If you eliminate even one group— for example, if you eliminate atheists—you eliminate the entire circle. The minute you've discarded one part of the whole, you've discarded the whole. And, in fact, a famous Jewish commentary on the importance of not killing says that he who saves just one life has saved the entire world.

As I said when I described the Net of Indra, each pearl reflects not just its neighboring pearl but all the pearls, the entire net. Each person, each phenomenon, contains our infinitely diverse universe.

A student of mine who is a Buddhist priest had a religious Catholic upbringing. As a young boy he learned that the consecrated Host inside the tabernacle in church was the body and blood of Christ, and he believed this completely. But as he grew up he stopped believing this. Instead, he felt that the consecrated Host was probably a symbol of the body and blood of Christ, but not the same thing. Almost fifty years later he told me this story: He did a solitary one-day retreat at a Franciscan church, sitting in his black priest's robes and facing the wall. Behind him was the tabernacle, and the red lit candle signified that it contained a consecrated

Host. Suddenly, as he sat there in meditation, he knew without a doubt that the consecrated Host in the tabernacle was indeed nothing other than the body and blood of Christ. This was not a memory of a teaching he'd received long ago but a sudden deep insight into the identity of the absolute and relative. He knew that the wafer lying in the tabernacle was not a symbol but actually was the unity of the world.

Some of us intuit this naturally. Sometimes we look at a snowflake, a flower, or a rock resting in the countryside and we see all of life. If we can deeply penetrate just one form of life, we can penetrate life in its totality. Every great artist knows this.

A common meditation practice is following one's breath. We sit still and follow our in-breath, then the out-breath, one after the other. If we give ourselves to this practice, if we become our inhalation and our exhalation, then there is nothing else. The infinite phenomena of the world are nothing other than this in-breath, this out-breath, and each breath is nothing other than the universe.

The vows to be oneness, diversity, and harmony comprise our basic orientation toward life. We steer our lives according to these values without even being conscious of it. Sometimes we live our lives according to one absolute, one big idea. We may even have a certain standard that causes us to be intolerant of other ideas and ways of life. At other times we see and appreciate the infinite variety of life in all of its manifestations but without any underlying unity. At that point we may feel no responsibility for anything, no reason to take action, to strive, or to take care of something. We can see a dry, thirsty lawn and appreciate its difference from thriving green grass without any thought of watering it. Unless we're grounded in unity, in I am you and you are me, we may have no incentive to act.

A peacemaker steers his life according to harmony. He sees the identity of the absolute and relative. Each person, each encounter, is nothing other than the oneness of life, nothing other than him. The Buddha is nothing other than the dried-out grass that's thirsty or the child crossing the street. Having taken the first three vows, we're in the realm of action. We take care of things. Not just any action, but intimate action. Action that comes out of connection, the knowledge that we are each and every sentient being in the universe. I am his leg and he is my arm. She is my fingers and I am her shoulder. Because we're so connected, we take action.

In Buddhism we call such action *compassion*. *Com-passion* means *with suffering*. Peacemaker action comes about when we are the suffering of others. When we are the hungry children, when we are a homeless mother, when we are the dying, when we are the inmates of a concentration camp. When we are Vietnamese villagers being strafed by helicopter machine guns, and when we're also the soldiers strafing the Vietnamese.

— 12 —

Claude Anshin Angyo Thomas

I was introduced to Claude Thomas in 1994 by another peacemaker priest, Michael O'Keefe. Claude was athletic (he'd been a martial arts teacher for years), and his back was heavily tattooed. He wore his long blond hair in a ponytail (although after he was ordained he has kept his head shaved).

From the very first meeting I had with Claude, I was struck by his tremendous openness and vulnerability. He could have remained silent about many things in his life, especially about the hurts he'd inflicted, both on himself and on others. But Claude held nothing back. This is what Claude told me about himself.

He was born and raised in a small rural town in Pennsylvania. He enlisted in the United States Army at the age of seventeen and was shipped to Vietnam. It was 1965. He was told he would be serving his country and the cause of freedom, and he believed what he was told. When he arrived in Vietnam he became a helicopter gunner. After a while he also became crew chief. He served on helicopter slickships, which carried troops to battle, and on gunships, which provided close fire support.

From the beginning Claude was thorough and highly disciplined. In the first months of his tour of duty, before going out on a mission, the twelve men in the three helicopter crews would pool their money and make bets on who would have the most confirmed kills that day. Claude sometimes won the pool. Because of the pool, he made sure to count how many people he killed on each mission, and that's how he knows that in less than a year he'd killed several hundred Vietnamese men, women, and children.

He was shot down five times. The last time he was shot down, which was somewhere in the Mekong Delta, he was gravely wounded: his shoulder and face shattered; his jaw, cheekbones, and ribs broken; his sternum split. "When I left Vietnam I was in a morphine haze. My neck was broken and the doctors were saying they would have to amputate my arm at the shoulder. At an evacuation hospital a nurse held my one good hand for twenty-four hours before I left. I never saw her face and I don't know her name."

He spent nine months in a military hospital in Kentucky. After he recuperated he flew home. While he was changing planes in Newark Airport in New Jersey, a woman saw him in his uniform, approached him, and spat in his face.

He went home, then to college, dropped out, became homeless, and couldn't get a job. Lots of drugs. "At night memories came—being shot down, the cries of the wounded. Screams of people I'd killed." He went to England and then to Iran because he'd heard drugs were cheap there. He was often violent. Once he was arrested by Savak, the shah's secret police, and interrogated and tortured for a few weeks. He returned to the United States and in 1983 went into a drug rehabilitation program and became a martial arts teacher, sitting in meditation before and after each class. In 1989 he stopped doing martial arts because of a growing commitment to nonviolence. But the memories and nightmares continued.

Then a social worker told him about a Vietnamese Zen monk who worked with Vietnam veterans. The monk's name was Thich Nhat Hanh. Thây (pronounced "Tai"), as he was called by students and associates, had worked hard for reconciliation with the North Vietnamese during the war and was famous for the social projects he'd undertaken in Vietnam, particularly around his home city of Hue. In the 1960s, Martin Luther King Jr. had nominated him for the Nobel Peace Prize. When the North Vietnamese came to power in Vietnam he was expelled as an enemy of the people and went into exile. He settled in France and built a community of mindfulness called Plum Village for his Vietnamese and Western followers. He also came to the United States regularly to work with war veterans. Claude met him in 1991 at a retreat at the Omega Institute in Rhinebeck, New York.

"He [Thây] walked into this room where I was sitting with other veterans and I felt I was face-to-face with the enemy, the Vietcong." Claude had thought of all Vietnamese as his enemies. Buddhist monks were no exception. Once, while serving in Vietnam, he was leaving a small Vietnamese village with four other American soldiers. Three Vietnamese men passed them wearing the saffron robes of Buddhist monks. After passing the American soldiers they turned around, pulled out guns, and fired. All five Americans, including Claude, were wounded. Three died.

But Thây told the veterans that their stories

about the war, their suffering, and the suffering of the Vietnamese people were very important. "You are the light at the tip of the candle," he told them. Their role was to expose the hurts of the war to an American public that wanted to ignore and forget them.

The other veterans at Omega put together the money for Claude to go to Plum Village in France, but it was painfully difficult for him to live with the Vietnamese, his old enemies. At first he could not do walking meditation because it brought on intense fear of being ambushed. Rather than living with the others, he pitched a tent in the woods in the countryside and booby-trapped the area. "I set up a base camp the way they'd trained me. Then I sat up on the trail every night because I was so afraid."

One evening they asked him to give a talk. Thây was there. After the talk he asked Claude to speak again at a retreat for two hundred helping professionals. After that Claude began to address groups of Vietnam veterans, social workers, and other professionals, and led days of mindfulness in the United States and Europe.

When I met Claude in 1994 I offered to ordain him as a peacemaker priest. He couldn't believe his ears. "You want to ordain me as a priest?" he asked. I said yes.

"What do you want me to do?"

"Just be Claude," I told him. "Keep on doing what you're doing."

It was then that we agreed that he would take the peacemaker vows in Auschwitz, at the beginning of his six-month walk, and that I would ordain him at the end, when he reached Vietnam. The month before our scheduled meeting in Vietnam my own teacher died. I took on new responsibilities and could not fly out to meet Claude. Three of my students flew out there instead and walked with him and his group as he visited past battle sites, bases where he'd been stationed, and the places where he'd been shot down. Thirty years after he left the country, it was still hard for Claude to speak to the Vietnamese, to forget that once these people had been his enemies. He began every day and ended every evening of that month-long walk with meditation.

Among the people who accompanied Claude to Vietnam was his son, Zach. When Claude originally returned from Vietnam he married and had a son. But whenever Zach cried as a baby and reached out to his father, Claude could not pick him up. He didn't know why. Only many years later he remembered. Once in Vietnam he and the three other members of his crew stood by their helicopter close to a village. As usual, many children came out to play with them and peer curiously at their helicopter. Suddenly Claude saw a baby in their midst. One of the American soldiers bent over to pick him up. Claude, too, started to step forward, froze, then stepped back. The baby exploded, killed along with two American soldiers. The baby had been booby-trapped.

Since ordaining Claude I've joined him at some of his retreats in Europe and he's joined me in street retreats in New York City's Bowery. I never fail to be moved by his interaction with others. His strength lies in his total self-exposure. He tells his story, not holding anything back, and in so doing he opens up a raw and vulnerable space other participants enter, where they feel safe enough to talk about their own personal pain, their own demons.

We once participated in an interfaith peace conference in Switzerland. As soon as Claude arrived he was told that two gangs had fought on the streets of Basel and that a teen member of one gang had shot a member of the other gang. Claude was asked if he would go to the jail and talk to the teenager who did the shooting. He agreed, but on condition that he be permitted to speak to all the members of both gangs. He left the conference, went to the jail in Basel, and talked to all the gang members involved. He spent the entire day with them, talking first with the teenager who did the shooting, then with the other gang members, then with the second gang, and finally with all of them together. By the end of the meeting the tough gang members asked him if he would come to live with them. The social worker who supervised this meeting said she'd never seen anyone relate to the gang members so directly and openly, without a hint of judgment. And Claude didn't even speak German.

"I've killed many people," Claude says. "I can't judge anybody." And he adds, "Anytime we kill—it doesn't matter for what reason—we not only create suffering in others, we suffer. We have to justify it to ourselves, and we do it on some level by deciding that the other person is not as human as we are."

Wherever Claude goes, his presence and message are essentially the same. He has borne witness to killing, and out of that has come his healing. In the process of making peace with himself he invites others to bear witness to their lives and sorrows, and out of that comes their healing.

— 13 —

I Vow to Penetrate
the Unknown

My wife, Jishu Holmes, is the cofounder of the Greyston Network in southwest Yonkers and has worked with me in developing the Greyston companies for many years. A former biochemist, she joined the Zen Community of New York in the early 1980s. She was ordained as a Buddhist priest and finally, after many years of study, became a Zen teacher.

Jishu served as controller of the Greyston Bakery when we started it in 1982 and then became the founder and executive director of the Greyston Family Inn, a housing complex for families with no homes. She started the child care center and designed a program of tenant services. Jishu did the preliminary program development for the housing and medical center for people with AIDS. And finally, before cofounding the Zen Peacemaker Order with me, she developed a new company to produce beautiful clothing and accessory items out of fabrics that are discarded by the big garment manufacturing companies, with the vision of hiring and training unemployed residents of the inner city. This combined her love of sewing with her deep belief that nothing is worthless, whether it's fabrics or human beings.

Altogether, Jishu spent some fifteen years of her

life working in Greyston. But one day I watched her come out of a tough meeting with other Greyston staff members. There were disagreement and disharmony among the various staff people, with no resolution in sight. Visibly disappointed and downhearted, she shook her head and said, "You know, after all the time I've spent working here, if there was one thing I thought I knew, it was Greyston. But when I came out of the meeting today I realized that after all these years I knew nothing about Greyston. Nothing at all."

Jishu's situation and her words capture for me the essence of our fourth peacemaker vow: to penetrate the unknown. Unknowing makes it possible for anything and everything to happen, to just pop up. When we don't know, when we have no expectations or fixed ideas about something, then everything that happens at any given moment is just what's happening.

But Jishu thought she knew. That's when her—and our—problems begin. As soon as we know something, we prevent something else from happening. When we live in a state of knowing, rather than unknowing, we're living in a fixed state of being where we can't experience the endless unfolding of life, one thing after another. Things happen anyway—nothing ever remains the same—but our notions of what *should* happen block us from seeing what actually *does* happen. We get upset because our expectations aren't met. When we can let go of them we are in accord with things as they arise.

We like to use the phrase "let it be." The truth is, we have no choice. No matter what we think, we are never in control and things will happen as they happen. But in a state of unknowing we actually live without attachment to preconceived ideas. There is no expectation of gain, no expectation of loss. There's just what's here right now.

For this reason I actively discourage candidates and members of the Peacemaker Order from asking questions that start with *why,* for those questions indicate a desire to know. They also reflect our fear or hesitation about dealing with something. In the order we practice living in a state of unknowing, not of knowing. This is very, very hard. Many of our members have spent years doing social action and have extensive knowledge in community development, ecology and the environment, education, the business world, psychology, social work, medicine, or the arts. In the past they believed that the way to become more effective was to know more. If they knew more about this or that, things would be different. But when they join the Zen Peacemaker Order they train in unknowing, in unlearning all their previous conditioning and preconceptions about how to make peace.

We don't ask them to discard their professional skills and knowledge. In fact, we actively encourage them to use all their expertise. And we help them develop the openness to see things as they are, the constant flow and interpenetration of life, free from expectation, boundary, and limit. In fact, a major operating principle of the order is: Study and practice are not two. We want to have knowledge, but not be controlled by knowledge.

And it's difficult. I trained for many years in Zen practice, which deals directly with the practice of unknowing, with my Japanese-born teacher in Los Angeles. Finally I became a teacher and moved to New

York to start the Zen Community of New York in Riverdale. One of the first retreats I led included a wonderful group of nuns who had maintained a strong meditation practice for many years as part of their Catholic vocation. They'd also worked for years with the poor in Jersey City, New Jersey. At the end of the retreat they asked me to join them for tea, which I did. While drinking tea they began to talk about their many years of meditation. They also talked of God.

Zen Buddhism, unlike many religious traditions, has no deity. Even its founder, Shakyamuni Buddha, the Enlightened One, is seen as an ordinary man who attained great enlightenment after years of practice. So as I listened to them talk I shook my head, thinking to myself, "They've been meditating for so long, and they still believe in God!"

As soon as that thought crossed my mind, I caught myself. Here I was, Bernie Glassman, and I *knew* that meditation had nothing to do with God. I was a young, relatively inexperienced Zen teacher, and already I *knew* that these nuns, who had practiced their rich vocation for so many years, were wrong to talk about God.

It's probably no accident that since that evening in 1979 I've worked extensively with people from many different traditions, religious and lay, and I've learned from them that there's no conflict between meditation practice and the worship of God. But that evening, even after many years of Zen studies, I still believed I knew. Just as my wife, Jishu, believed she knew the Greyston organizations. Whenever you know, you've reached a dead end.

As a Zen teacher, I've worked with students

who gained wonderful insights and clarity out of their meditation practice. And I've also seen them hang on to those insights. The happier they feel, the more they hang on. It's human to cling to something that feels good, but by holding on to a past experience they don't experience this very moment, this—NOW!

The minute we gain something—insight, knowledge, or understanding—we must be ready to let it go and return to the state of unknowing. Without that we can't go further.

As the founder of the Greyston Mandala, I receive hundreds of letters from people asking me questions about how we developed our organizations and what they should learn from us. I'm always glad to share information with them; in fact, I've traveled all over the country and given talks on our Greyston model. But I always end by telling people that I don't know what they should do. Things will happen to them that didn't happen to us. If they develop expectations based on our experience without cultivating the state of unknowing, openings and opportunities will arise that they won't see.

All of us have different ingredients with which to cook a meal. That meal can be anything: a business project, a family outing, a new company, a work of art. Whatever meal we cook will depend on the ingredients at hand. The less we know, the more open we'll be to the ingredients we have and the more creative will be our cooking. If I know that a white powder on the table is salt I won't see the possibility that it may be flour, sugar, or rat poison. Or I'll look enviously at ingredients other people have instead of making the best possible meal I can make out of my own ingredients. But if I don't know, I'll explore, I'll taste, I'll experiment. I'll be more free and creative with my cooking.

When we penetrate the unknown we don't see the meal, we see the ingredients. That's what I meant when I wrote in the prologue that this book won't give you answers to how to make peace; instead, it describes the ingredients of peacemaking. And one of the most important ingredients in cooking the meal of peace, as in cooking any meal, is unknowing.

As I've said, one of my constant challenges as a Zen teacher is to develop new practices to keep students in the state of unknowing. There are many ways of doing this. For instance, when we were at Auschwitz-Birkenau, people went into shock that first day, which is a form of unknowing. The reality of the place surpassed their expectations to such an extent that their regular habits of self-centered thoughts and opinions no longer operated as before. It was only then that we began to sit in our bearing witness circle around the train tracks.

You don't have to go as far as Auschwitz to be in a state of unknowing. Claude Thomas's first teacher, Thich Nhat Hanh, uses a bell of mindfulness to bring his students' awareness back to the present moment. In the present moment there are no thoughts, no concepts, just—THIS!

Similarly, at the stroke of noon every day members of the Zen Peacemaker Order stop what they're doing for one minute of silent meditation for world peace. I've been doing this practice for many, many years. Can you imagine what would happen if all the people in the world stopped what they were doing every day at noon and returned to the present moment? Can you imagine what would happen if all of us lived in the present moment, in the state of the unknown, every moment of every day?

Yet we still want to know. In some way we can't help it—we're human. As part of being human, we believe that the reason we're not happy or not successful is that somewhere in the world there is a piece of knowledge we haven't acquired yet. If we can find it with the help of the right book, the right religion, the right teacher, or the right job, we'll be happy and successful.

The practice at the Zen Peacemaker Order is one of letting go. Not letting go of the things we know but of our attachment to them. This is an important distinction. Since we wish to make peace in all areas of life, we need to make use of every tool possible, each bit of knowledge and technological advance. What we want is Hotei's bag. Hotei is a Zen Buddhist character in the last of a famous series of pictures about the road to enlightenment. The quest is long and arduous. The final picture shows Hotei returning to the marketplace carrying a bag over his shoulder. He is ready to work with all people and with whatever comes up. His bag contains everything he'll ever need. So if he meets a beggar he reaches into his bag and takes out coins. If he finds a child lying sick on the road he reaches into his bag and takes out a bandage. If he encounters a garden full of weeds he takes out a rake and a hoe.

As peacemakers we also want to carry Hotei's bag wherever we go, and we want it to contain everything we'll ever need. So if we encounter a person with AIDS we'll give him medication. If we meet a family with no place to go we'll find them a home. We want to have as much knowledge and as many resources as possible, but unless we approach the situation from a state of unknowing we won't know what to reach for. If we meet a heroin addict we could take him to a detox unit. Or we could give him a new needle to prevent HIV infection. If we see a prostitute soliciting in Times Square on a snowy night we could tell her to stop. Or we could give her a cup of hot coffee to keep her warm. Or we could give her a condom to keep her safe. Hotei's bag contains all these things. What we reach for in the bag will depend on our preconceptions and judgments. The fewer ideas we have about right or wrong, good or bad, the more natural and spontaneous will be our responses. When we let go of our ideas about how to fix ourselves and others, we'll know naturally what to take out of our bag.

The vow to penetrate the unknown is similar to step 3 of AA and other twelve-step recovery programs: We make a decision to turn over our wills and our lives to the care of God as we understand Him. This step is taken by people who lived their lives according to what they knew. They knew they weren't alcoholics; they knew they could stop drinking whenever they wished. By the time they take step 3 they've admitted that they're alcoholics. They realize that whatever they've tried hasn't worked out and that they have no control over their lives—that, in fact, they don't really know.

Unknowing is essential to anyone in recovery. It's also essential to peacemakers. At the same time that we accumulate knowledge and experience, we need to wipe the slate clean and be in a state of unknowing. For only then can we bear witness.

— 14 —

I Vow to Bear Witness

In the early months of 1997, Claude Thomas came back from a month of retreats in Europe. He came down to Yonkers from his hometown of Concord, Massachusetts, and as usual, told me stories about what had happened to him in Europe.

Telling peacemaking stories is one of the most important ingredients in the order. We tell stories that are true and stories that we wish were true. We tell the straight facts as we know them, and we also tell the myths of our lives, tales that reflect our deepest dreams and yearnings. Finally, there are what I call our black-and-white stories, those that get told between the lines: the things that are left unsaid, the shadow behind our public statements. Whether they tell the facts, whether they're made up, or whether they're told in silence, they're all peacemaking stories. And they're all true, for they reflect how we see ourselves and the world. So we share them whenever we get together.

This is one of the stories that Claude told me:

He had just returned from Belgium, where the people and the media were preoccupied with the case of a man who had abducted six girls, kept them in an underground cellar, and sexually abused them. The police eventually caught him, but not before four of the girls had starved to death. Subsequently, a major political scandal erupted in Belgium over the ineffectiveness of the police and the legal system, culminating with a silent candlelight march of 300,000 people in the streets of Brussels.

The mother of one of the girls who died resided near the retreat center where Claude came to speak. After his first public talk someone in the audience asked him if he would speak to this woman, and he agreed.

The girl's mother talked to him for two hours. She talked about the horrible death of her young daughter. She talked without stop about her pain, her grief, her anger, and her overwhelming loss. She cried. She talked about the anger she felt toward the killer. Claude understood her anger, and he also knew that he had killed many young girls in Vietnam. He said to her, "How can you most acknowledge your child? Is it in executing this man, or by helping change society so that this kind of man doesn't arise again?"

She said, "But he was responsible."

Claude said, "I know he was responsible. I was responsible for the deaths of children in Vietnam and to this day I still don't sleep because of that."

As they talked it became clear that this mother did not really hate the man who had killed her child. In fact, she was able to feel his suffering. She said that no one could do what he had done unless there was terrible hurt deep inside. She'd tried to say this to her friends and family, but they couldn't hear it. Claude heard it. Later he told me, "I felt not only her grief and her loss, I also felt the suffering of her daughter and of the man who'd killed her. I felt all of them."

In my view, we can't heal ourselves or other people unless we bear witness. In the Zen Peacemaker Order we stress bearing witness to the wholeness of life, to every aspect of the situation that arises. So bearing witness to someone's kidnapping, assaulting, and killing a child means being every element of the situation: being the young girl, with her fear, terror, hunger, and pain; being the killer, with his rage and hurt; being the girl's mother, with her endless nights of grief and guilt; being the mother of the man who killed, torn between love for her son and the horror of his actions; being the families of both the killed and the killer, each with its respective pain, anger, horror, and shame; being the dark, silent cell where the girl was imprisoned; being the police officers who finally, under enormous pressure, caught the man; and being the jail cell holding the convicted man. It means being each and every element of this situation.

You can see immediately how hard this is. Sometimes all we can do, at least in the beginning, is bear witness to our own rage. This woman extended her boundaries. She bore witness not only to herself and her own grief, but also to her child's killer.

And what does it mean to be a murdered young girl, her mother, her killer, the killer's mother, and a policeman? It means that at that moment there is no separation between that person and me. In Zen practice, when we do deep meditation, our identity and ego structure dissolve. Over time our minds become more transparent and therefore more spacious, with less attachment to any ideas and preconceptions about who we are. In that state we discover our oneness with life. We see that we are not just who we thought previously, we're the entire universe. Every creature, every person, every phenomenon is just another aspect of who we are. A little girl, a mother, a killer, and a policeman are all aspects of who we are. So is the nightingale, the hawk that kills the nightingale, and the hunter who kills the hawk. We are the victims, the perpetrators, and the people who stand indifferently by. We are the feelings and thoughts of all these people, who are nothing other than aspects of ourselves. We are not attracted or repelled, for we are them.

Recently I had a conversation with a good friend, the actress Ellen Burstyn. In our discussions about bearing witness, she told me about her own training at the Actors Studio. She said that whenever she rehearses for a role, she looks for the person she's trying to be inside herself. If she plays a mother, she tries to find the mother in herself; if a grandmother, she tries to find the grandmother in herself. And if she plays a healer, a dying person, or a mass murderer, she finds that person in herself as well. That approach assumes that we have it in us to be every person and everything in the world—from Mother Teresa to Adolf Hitler.

The approach in Zen practice is based on penetrating the unknown, on starting out with no concepts or ideas about how a killer, or his young victim, might behave. Either way, we are bearing witness to parts of ourselves that we ordinarily ignore—and often avoid. We become the terror and gnawing hunger of the starving girl, the grief of her mother, the explosive rage and fear of the killer, the distress and shame of his mother. By allowing them to emerge, we are re-membering, reconnecting, with those parts of ourselves. It's the beginning of making ourselves—and society—whole.

Earlier I quoted the famous Jewish prayer Shema Yisrael: "Listen O Israel, the Lord our God, the Lord is One." The Buddhist service that we perform on the streets of New York City's Bowery begins: "Attention! Attention!" When we say "Listen O Israel" what do we mean? When we say "Attention!" what do we mean? When we really listen, when we really pay attention to the sounds of joy and suffering in the universe, then we are not separate from them, we become them. Because in reality we are not separate from those who suffer. We are them; they are us. It is our suffering, and it is our joy. When we don't listen, we are shutting ourselves off—not from others but from ourselves.

We can't do any of this from a place of knowing. When we think we know something, we don't listen. We have to empty ourselves over and over, return to unknowing, and just listen. And listen. And listen.

Listening means seeing the ingredients in front of us. Everything we see and hear is an ingredient of ourselves. If we can listen not just with our ears but with our eyes, our noses, our mouths, and every pore of our bodies, then we not only see all the ingredients in front of us, we *are* those ingredients.

And once we listen, we have to act. The functioning that comes out of listening—out of "Attention!"—is compassionate action. If we don't listen, we can't act with compassion.

I don't believe that any of us can bear witness fully to any situation, and certainly not to all situations. The important thing is to try to look a little more broadly than just at our own individual suffering, as the

Belgian mother did when she spoke to Claude. The wider your point of view, the more you bear witness. And out of that bearing witness a healing will arise. Bearing witness brings us into loving action, the goal of which is to reduce suffering.

Bearing witness is essential to the training in the Zen Peacemaker Order. We bear witness on the streets of the Bowery in New York City. We encourage our members not just to train in hospices but also to work in funeral homes so that they can see how we look when we're dead and are being prepared for burial or cremation. One member recently told me he'd like to work as a geriatric counselor in an old-age home. I told him that was fine but if he wished to bear witness, he might look into signing himself in as a patient.

This is an important distinction. Most of our peacemakers have had extensive experience in social action. But that doesn't mean they've borne witness. If they're helping professionals they know how to help but not necessarily how to be helped. They may not know what it is to have physical needs that are not met, to be ignored, or to be treated as a patient rather than as a human being. They've gone down to the Bowery to give food to the hungry, but they often don't know what it's like to receive food on the streets. And if they've worked with prison inmates or started halfway houses, they haven't done this from the inside, like Fleet Maull. Fleet is in the middle of a twenty-five-year prison sentence for drug-related crimes. While doing time in the federal penitentiary he bore witness to those dying in prison and began a prison hospice network in prisons across the United States and Canada.

I will say more about Fleet later in the book. We

can't all go to prison in order to do work with inmates and we can't all die in order to work with the dying. But in a sense we do die. We die to our limited views of ourselves, awaken to our boundless unity with the universe, and bear witness.

Finally, I wish to talk about the opposite of bearing witness, which is denial. The best story I know about denial is the story of the early life of the founder of Buddhism, Shakyamuni Buddha. When the Buddha was born in India some 2,500 years ago, a great seer told his father, the king of the Shakya tribe, that his son would be either a great king who would unite all the Indian tribes under his rule or a great spiritual leader. The king wished his son to be a great king rather than a spiritual leader, so after the child was born he kept him inside a beautiful palace. The palace had everything that the prince wanted, including every comfort and luxury the world could offer. But the sick and the old were not permitted in the palace. Nor was the prince permitted to go outside the palace walls.

He grew up, married a beautiful princess, and they had a son. But he grew restless. He wanted to see what was outside the walls of his palace. Finally he persuaded his charioteer to take him out of the palace secretly one night. That first night they encountered a sick man lying on the road. The young prince had never seen such a thing and asked the charioteer what it was. The charioteer replied, "This is illness." They returned to the palace and the Buddha considered what he had seen. The following night he persuaded the charioteer to take him outside the palace once again. This time they found an old man on the road. The Buddha had never seen this either and asked the charioteer what it was. The charioteer said, "This is old age." Again they returned to the palace and the Buddha pondered what he had seen. The following night they again left the palace. This time they encountered a dead man on the road. The Buddha asked what this was, and the charioteer replied, "This is death."

The prince returned to the palace. By now he was overwhelmed. He'd never encountered illness, old age, and death before. He grew more and more restless. The things that had once given pleasure were now meaningless. He saw his life for what it was, a life behind walls. The sights he'd seen had aroused questions he'd never asked himself. And he didn't know how to answer them.

One last time he urged his charioteer to take him out of the palace. This time they saw a mendicant on the road. The Buddha asked his charioteer what this was. The charioteer replied that this was a spiritual seeker who had renounced the world in order to find the meaning of life. The prince returned home. Finally he knew what he had to do.

One night, after everyone had gone to sleep, he left the palace. In the forest, he removed his royal clothing, jewelry, and sword. Shedding every trace of his old identity, he put on the rags of a mendicant.

This is a story about denial. It is not only about the Buddha's royal father, it is about every father and mother who wish to spare their children any contact with want or pain. When their children grow into adulthood and are confronted by these things, both in their own lives and in the lives of others, they don't know what to do, so they look away.

As a society, we wish to deny the existence of

the very things the Buddha's father wished to conceal from his son. So we turn away from the homeless, from the alcoholic, from the poor, from the diseased, from the dying, from the beggar on the street. Just like the prince, we live behind walls that block out sights we don't wish to see. In order to see them, we too have to go beyond those walls.

The training and practice at the Peacemaker Order is to witness. Not to deny, but to broaden, our vision. Not to teach but to listen. It's an ever-deepening, never-ending practice. And it starts and ends with unknowing. We don't bear witness to tell other people what to do with their lives. After many years of study, teaching, and peacemaking, I realized that I was deluded, that I would always be deluded, that I will never get to a place where I know, and that therefore I will penetrate the unknown and bear witness forever. And that means bearing witness, letting go, bearing witness, letting go, bearing witness, and letting go.

The Buddha searched for the truth, for enlightenment, for many years. Finally, at the town of Magadha, he sat under a tree and vowed never to get up until his search had ended. By the time the morning star had risen, his search had indeed ended. There are many tales of what happened to him that night. The one I like best relates how Mara, the lord of illusion, flung illusions of all kinds at the Buddha, sitting beneath the tree. He began with monsters and demons. As each apparition approached him, the Buddha said, "This is me." And Mara sent famine, flood, fire, earthquake, and to these, too, the Buddha said, "This is me." Finally, at the very end, Mara sent his daughters, the most beautiful women in the world, to the Buddha. And as he watched them approach, the Buddha never budged, but only said, "This is me." Finally Mara gave up. He had thrown at the Buddha every situation that life could present, and instead of running back to his father's palace the Buddha had simply said, "This is me."

Each and every one of us was raised in a palace surrounded by walls. In those very things that we most deny lies the greatest energy for healing. But first we must bear witness: to AIDS, to poverty, to hunger. To rivers, to mountains, to a laughing child. To war, to Auschwitz, to the morning star. By saying "This is me."

— 15 —

I Vow to Heal Myself and Others

It's a myth that spiritual people are not attached, that they're somehow above the trials and tribulations of ordinary life. Not only are they affected by things, they're tremendously affected by them. For rather than living in the realm of ideas and feelings about suffering, they live in the realm of action.

How do they know what action to take? How do they know how to heal?

When we bear witness, when we become the situation—homelessness, poverty, illness, violence, death—the right action arises by itself. We don't have to worry about what to do. We don't have to figure out solutions ahead of time. Peacemaking is the functioning of bearing witness. Once we listen with our entire body and mind, loving action arises.

Loving action is right action. It's as simple as giving a hand to someone who stumbles or picking up a child who has fallen on the floor. We take such direct, natural actions every day of our lives without considering them special. And they're not special. Each is simply the best possible response to that situation in that moment.

In the Zen Peacemaker Order we commit ourselves to healing others at the same time that we heal ourselves. We don't wait to be peaceful before we begin to make peace. In fact, when we see the world as one body, it's obvious that we heal everyone at the same time that we heal ourselves, for there are no "others."

Many years ago in Los Angeles I had an experience in which I felt—I saw—the suffering of hungry spirits. I was surrounded by all kinds of suffering beings. Almost immediately I made a vow to serve them, to feed them. But how do we feed them? How do we feed ourselves? We, too, are hungry spirits. We, too, are suffering beings. How do we feed everyone and everything in the universe? How do we heal ourselves and our society?

This question has been my life. In the beginning I believed that a diligent meditation practice was the answer. In fact, I was a fanatic about meditation and retreats. I thought that if I persevered I would become enlightened, like Shakyamuni Buddha 2,500 years ago. If I concentrated hard enough, I'd eventually experience what he experienced. And then I would go out and take action.

It took me a long time to understand that I couldn't wait till then to take action. That understanding, too, came out of bearing witness. I became a Zen teacher, founded the Zen Community of New York, and for the next fifteen years developed the group of community development companies called the Greyston Mandala. We didn't follow a blueprint; in fact, we were constantly being told that we didn't know what we were doing.

In the beginning we needed a livelihood for the community, so we started operating a for-profit bakery. The Greyston Bakery was located in the inner city of southwest Yonkers while we ourselves lived in the affluent neighborhood of Riverdale, three miles to the south. When the business expanded and we began to hire neighborhood residents, we ran into new issues and concerns that we hadn't had before: absenteeism, chronic lateness, lack of basic work skills. So we dug deeper. We talked to our employees, we walked the neighborhood with them, and we saw it with their eyes. Finally we left Riverdale and moved into southwest Yonkers ourselves.

What we saw was the lack of affordable homes. Many of our employees lived with uncles and cousins in small, cramped apartments, always on the verge of being kicked out. Some actually lived in a shelter three blocks away, with no homes of their own. We also noticed the lack of child care. Our female employees often brought their children to the bakery, though this was illegal, because there was no one to take care of their children during the day. We saw the lack of basic work skills when some of the employees couldn't measure the necessary ingredients and we ended up throwing away large quantities of unusable cake batter. We witnessed violence and addiction when people didn't show up for work on account of drug use or alcohol. On occasion we found out that they'd been shot or stabbed.

After bearing witness to this over several years, one day after another, and given all the ingredients we had on hand, the right actions soon became obvious. We started pre-job and on-the-job bakery training programs. They included classes in basic life and work skills, including arithmetic and measurement. Then, over time, we started Greyston Family Inn, with permanent housing for families with no homes, and a child care center. After the tenants moved in they taught us more about what was needed: literacy tutors and after-school programs for school-age children, with classes on parenting, money management, and tenant issues for the adults.

Greyston is still confronted by new issues all the time. The manager of the Greyston Bakery says that every day brings with it new questions and problems. You might think that since we've been in this neighborhood for so long we'd know how to take care of things. But the ingredients change and we bear witness again and again.

Our biggest teachers have been our own neighbors and employees. By living and working at their side the right actions arise. Moslems, Buddhists, Jews, and Pentecostals all live together on one block. We share with them the problems that afflict American inner cities. There has been violence in our community, including robbery, assault, and even homicide. But we also have joint celebrations and block association meetings to discuss how to keep our neighborhood clean and drug-free. When the weather is warm we begin the mornings by picking up the trash around the block. These are small actions that arise out of bearing witness.

Similarly, when Jishu and I decided to found the Zen Peacemaker Order, we followed no blueprint. Instead we adopted the Three Tenets as the basic guidelines for the order. Everything we did was based on them, including the formation of the order, our training programs, and even, as you will see further on, funding for the order.

And it begins with the state of unknowing, with the vow to let go of our conditioned responses and penetrate the unknown. In the Peacemaker Order we don't ask ourselves what are the right methods of handling conflict. Instead we try to approach the situation with no attachment to ideas or solutions. Only then can we really bear witness. And as we become each situation that arises, as we find in ourselves the place of suffering, illness, or despair, the healing arises.

The broader the bearing witness, the broader and more powerful the healing that will take place. As peacemakers, the action we take in any situation will reflect our understanding of the different aspects of that situation, the extent to which we're able to bear witness to them, and consequently, who we are. If we truly believe that we are all one body, if we truly bear witness to that one body, then we won't neglect anyone.

At Auschwitz, before we could bear witness to what had happened there many years ago we had to bear witness to each other and to the differences among us. As we did that, an intimacy arose naturally and spontaneously. As we listened to each other, we began to take care of one another. At the same time, an intimacy arose between ourselves and Auschwitz. The names we chanted became our own. The barbed wire felt softer with time. Love came back to us from ruined barracks that before we couldn't bear to enter.

Of itself the fruit is born. Each of us is that fruit. Claude Thomas, who bears witness to killing, is that fruit. The Belgian mother who bore witness to the pain of her daughter's killer, she is that fruit. We bear witness and the fruit is born, the Supreme Meal is offered. What is this Supreme Meal? The life of each and every one of us.

— 16 —

Continuous Practice

We start from the unknown, we bear witness, and healing arises. Then we let go of what we've seen and learned and begin the cycle all over again. It's a continuous practice.

The next moment is never going to be the same. The ingredients will be different. What worked once won't necessarily work the next time. What caused transformation in the past won't necessarily cause it again. We must return to the unknown and look again at our ingredients, for they will have changed. And therefore today's meal will be different from yesterday's, and also different from tomorrow's.

This sounds logical, but it's actually hard to accept. We like to think that finally there is an end. We like to think that somewhere in the world there is a magic trick that will work every time. In fact, the better something works one time, the harder it is to let go of it. Things become particularly dangerous when we have succeeded. Once we have a deep and wonderful experience of healing, accompanied by sensations of peace and joy, it's very hard to drop it and start all over again. But if we don't, it will condition us to act in ways that are not appropriate for the next day, for the next healing process.

I remember well one of the phrases that we recited at Auschwitz each time we chanted the Kaddish in English: "Though we bless, praise, beautify, and offer up your name, Name that is Holy, Blessed One, still you remain beyond the reach of our praise, our song, beyond the reach of all consolation. Beyond! Beyond! And say, Yes. Amen."

We once chanted that service while standing in the area where people were forced to undress before being driven into the gas chamber. It is a long rectangular room built underground and people had to descend through a small entrance and down the steps. Some of us stood there, but some stood above and looked down; it was almost too intimate to go down the steps into that large undressing room. After we finished and I went up the steps I saw Rabbi Don Singer. He looked straight into my eyes and said, "It's beyond consolation. It's beyond consolation. Beyond! Beyond!"

No matter what we did at Auschwitz, no matter what services we recited, what interfaith forms we developed, no matter what we said in the small groups in the mornings and in the large group at night, no matter how great the love and healing that arose, Auschwitz itself was beyond consolation. What had happened there was beyond words, beyond forms, even beyond silence. Simply Beyond.

That is not to say that a great healing didn't arise during our time there. No one who heard the children of Nazis speak, who heard exchanges between Jews and Poles, or who watched us sit in the snow for five days could deny that something very important was happening. A doctor who participated in the retreat later wrote me these words: "What I continue to experience is a deeper connection with humanity. I have felt a sense of peace and serenity I didn't know possible. It is very confusing because I can't figure out how a place of extraordinary horror could transmute such powerful and subtle healing."

And in the mornings we always went back to Birkenau. Back to the unknown, to the unfathomable, to the place beyond consolation. We returned to our circle once more to bear witness. Each time we did that our hearts broke and the tears flowed as we listened to each other and to Auschwitz. By the end of the day there was a healing, and the following morning we returned to Birkenau. Again and again. For Auschwitz was beyond oneness, beyond diversity, simply, as the Kaddish says, Beyond.

Not only is Auschwitz beyond form, beyond consolation, so is everything in life. "What is the virtue of remaining hidden?" asked the Jewish woman who wished to leave Auschwitz that first night. Everything is hidden, nothing can be captured in form. The moment we try to define it—in word, in thought, in song—we've lost it. The forms hadn't been created that could deal with Auschwitz, she said, and so she wished to leave.

As a Zen teacher, I'd spent many years penetrating the world of no-form, the world of unknowing, the world of oneness. But bearing witness is about form. It's about practicing in the world of forms, of infinite differences and diversity. And so, rather than leaving, I've returned to Auschwitz several times. Each time I'm there I'm shocked once again. All words are stripped from me, I'm pushed into the unknown. In that state

I see and listen more deeply, and a healing arises. And the next morning—or the next year—I return to Auschwitz, to the world beyond consolation, and begin all over again.

Because it's a continuous practice.

PART III

BEARING WITNESS
ON
THE STREETS

Bernie Glassman twirling his walking stick on retreat in Penn Station, New York City, 1996.

—17—

The Unknown on
the Streets

I've told the story many times. After graduating from
the Polytechnic Institute of Brooklyn in 1960 I sat in a
pizza parlor (pizza is my favorite food) with a friend of
mine one day talking about what we'd do with our
lives. Then and there I made three vows: I was going to
live on an Israeli kibbutz; I was going to study in a Zen
monastery in Japan; and I was going to live on the
streets.

I ended up fulfilling each of these vows, though
in ways I never imagined. I spent some time in a kibbutz in Israel not too long after that conversation in the
pizza parlor. I also studied Zen for many years with a
Japanese Zen teacher in downtown Los Angeles, with
practice for short periods of time in monasteries in
Japan. Subsequently, most of my teaching time has been
spent in the inner city of southwest Yonkers.

As a Zen student and teacher, I lived with my
family in a communal setting with other Zen practitioners. Rarely did we have our own separate quarters.
When we did have our own house we were always surrounded by students, associates, guests, and fellow
workers. We were never alone.

And still I hadn't lived on the streets.

I began to think about doing a retreat on the

streets of the Bowery in 1987, shortly after we decided to build apartments for homeless families who were then living in Westchester motels. I remembered my vow from twenty-seven years earlier. I wanted to be one with people living on the streets, and the way to do that was to live on the streets. That did not mean I was homeless. In fact, from the very beginning I made a rule for myself and for those who joined me: If anybody ever asked us what we were doing on the streets of New York City, we would tell the truth: We were social activists living on the streets for several days. We were not homeless.

I finally did my first street retreat in 1991, four years later. And when our group of fifteen first assembled in the Cathedral of St. John the Divine in New York City that April day, in old clothes and a week's growth of beard, even then I had no idea what was going to happen or why I was doing it except that I was fulfilling a vow I'd made as a very young man.

Since then I've done annual street retreats on the Bowery, usually during Holy Week but also at other times of the year. I've gone on the streets in Zurich, Cologne, and Düsseldorf. A student of mine has taken people to live on the streets of Seattle, and not a week passes without inquiries from people and media about coming with me onto the streets or asking me to lead street retreats around the country.

After all these years I still don't completely understand why street retreats are such powerful experiences for everyone who participates. I do know that they have become very important practices for me and for members of the order and that they have profoundly influenced the way I think about training and practice.

It all has to do with unknowing and bearing witness.

Back in 1991, my friend, the Very Reverend James Morton, said it best. Jim Morton was then the dean of the Cathedral of St. John the Divine and he invited us to gather in his office at the cathedral on our way down to Central Park. Many years ago Jim had sent clergy members out to live on the streets of Chicago as part of their training. They called it "taking the plunge." I liked that phrase so much that years later, when we began the Zen Peacemaker Order, "plunge" became our name for those training programs, like street retreats, when we sent members and candidates into an uncertain and unpredictable situation.

I had arranged for us to meet some formerly homeless people who were working in one of the cathedral's programs. We asked them what we could expect and they gave us some very practical suggestions. They told us to stay away from shelters due to the danger of contracting tuberculosis. They said that if we had to sleep on the streets, we should head for Chinatown, where there was some possibility the cops wouldn't chase us away. They reminded us to keep our shoes on even while sleeping so that they wouldn't disappear in the middle of the night. But Jim Morton told us the most important thing.

"You'll learn the most from the unknown," he said. "The things you don't expect will come up and they will be your teacher."

He was right. Many, many things have come up

during the street retreats I've done since 1991, and they've all been unexpected. Whether we slept in Central Park or on wet pavements in Chinatown, whether we ate in the Bowery Mission downtown or at the Franciscan mission on West Thirty-first Street, in a Zurich park in May or on the steps of the U.S. Capitol in Washington, D.C., in a frigid January, at Easter or at Passover, inside subway cars or near a shantytown under the Manhattan Bridge, the unexpected always happened. It was our greatest teacher.

— 18 —

Begging

A street retreat starts long before the day we leave our homes and walk down to the Bowery. For some people it starts a month before; for others, six months before. You see, people accompany me on the streets on one condition: They have to beg. And they start their begging before the retreat by assembling a *mala*.

Malas are strings of beads worn as bracelets or necklaces, somewhat like Catholic rosaries. I require each retreat participant to assemble a *mala* of eighteen small beads, at a price of $108 each, and one large one, at a price of $1,080. The rule is that they can't pay for the beads themselves. They have to get nineteen people—family, friends, business associates—to buy a bead before they can go on the streets. The money goes to pay for projects of the Zen Peacemaker Order. I decided on the number 18 because it's the numerical equivalent of the Hebrew word for *Life*. I picked the number 108 because in the Hindu tradition there are 108 names of God and in the Buddhist tradition there are 108 types of delusions.

I will say more about the practice of assembling *malas,* or asking for money, later in the book. For now, let me acknowledge that requiring people to raise over $3,000 so that they can live on the streets for five days with no money in their pockets may seem somewhat paradoxical. In fact, some people call it outrageous.

In fact, some people call the entire practice of going on the streets outrageous. Over the years I've been told that street retreats were condescending and disrespectful of homeless people. Some have said that since none of us were really homeless, we wouldn't learn much from being on the streets for five days. Some have called it slumming; others have said it was gimmicky.

A Swiss social worker in Zurich once asked me how much food, clothing, and blankets we bring with us to give homeless people when we're on the streets. When I told him that we bring nothing with us, and that instead of bringing things we actually end up needing the same things street people need, his mouth fell open. "Then I don't understand you," he said. "If you don't bring anything with you, what are you doing?"

A Korean Buddhist monk I know worked for many years with teenagers who were classified as mentally retarded. Together, they built a temple in Korea and he ordained them as Buddhist monks. People thought he was crazy. What did it mean to ordain young people who were mentally retarded? What was he giving them? He replied that he was giving them nothing, for there was nothing to give, they were all Buddhas, all enlightened beings. And then he added, "In the Buddha's eyes, we are all retarded."

I tell this story not to draw a parallel between street people and the mentally retarded, simply to clarify our own actions. We don't go on the streets to bring things to people or to convince them to change their lives. There's nothing to bring and no one to change. There are simply the issues of eating, sleeping, peeing, defecating, and staying warm and dry—all while living on the streets

And still, many people tell me that going on the streets is crazy. And in some way they're right, it is crazy. What I like to do is put holes in people's paradigms. As part of teaching the practice of unknowing, I try to push people toward the experience of certain things rather than their concept of them. Whenever I do that it creates problems with the concepts. When our paradigms and concepts stop making sense, we get upset.

Let me give you a small example. When we first began to develop the Zen Peacemaker Order I coined the phrase *Servant-Warrior* to describe the role of certain activists and teachers in the order. But people objected, saying that *servant* was fine but *warrior* was not. *Warrior* implied war; it implied aggression and death. Certain members wanted to have nothing to do with that word. Worst of all, they said, the two didn't go together. According to our usual concepts, *servant* means one thing and *warrior* means something very different. People weren't ready to look at how the two might work together, how one individual could combine certain qualities of both to become a very powerful peacemaker. They thought the term was outrageous.

So is my asking people to raise money so that they can be penniless on the streets. Most people think there's something wrong with a person who begs on the street. They look at him and ask, or at least wonder, Why doesn't he get a job? We're trained to believe that working is the way to get money. When we see someone asking for it, a question, a doubt, appears in our mind: What's going on here? If we stay with that question for a long time, rather than continuing about our business, a shift will happen in our thinking. Our lives will change.

Heinz-Juergen Metzger, a resident of Germany who is associated with the Peacemaker Order, asked me to do a street retreat in his country. I agreed, on the condition that participants raised money from their friends and assembled *malas*. Heinz immediately responded that in Germany this was not done. In Germany, he explained, people were accustomed to their government's taking care of everything. That's why they paid high taxes. Private giving was not as common as in America. And buying a bead on someone's *mala* so that he or she could go on the streets for a week would be considered completely crazy. So I advised him to do it anyway.

Three months later he called. He'd finished assembling his *mala*. In the process of doing so he not only changed his own thinking about what is possible in Germany, he also raised a great many questions in the heads of the people from whom he begged. Some thought it was outrageous and gave him nothing. Others thought the same thing and started thinking about it. The situation didn't make sense, so they talked to him some more. Some of them gave him money, others didn't. It was a very interesting experience, he told me.

As a teacher of peacemakers, I see my role as putting people into that questioning mind, the mind of doubt, the mind of unknowing, again and again. A wealthy Greyston supporter, an elderly man, once joined us on the streets. As usual, I told him he would have to assemble a *mala* by asking his friends for money.

He asked, "How much does the total come to?"

I told him.

He said, "I'll write you a check."

"I won't take your check," I told him. "You have to go to your friends and ask them to give the money."

"That's crazy," he said. "I'm the one people come to when they need money. I never go and ask them."

Of course it was crazy; that was why I asked him to do it. I didn't want him to behave according to his norm, which was giving money. I wanted him to behave against the norm, and ask.

This is a big problem for a lot of people. Many have heard of our street retreats and ask if they can join. I would say that most of them don't come with us because they are reluctant to ask their friends and family for money. They're ready to give twenty times over, but not to ask. Just as they're ready to bring food and blankets to street people any night of the week, but not to have to ask for food and blankets for themselves. Asking—begging—is not the norm.

But behaving according to your norm doesn't cause a shift anyplace. That's why Mother Teresa once said at a private benefit that you have to give till it hurts. You have to give so much that you start to think about it, and then you have to give even more till it challenges your paradigms, your norms. That's the only way change comes about.

I remember attending a Jewish wedding in

Brooklyn. After the ceremony we sat down to dinner. It was a very Orthodox affair, with the men seated on one side of the room and the women on the other. Almost immediately a stream of Orthodox Jews, many of them rabbis, came by the table asking for money for various causes: schools, synagogues, brides' dowries, and so on. They came one after another, stopping by the guests seated around the table, and each guest put his hand into his pocket and gave them money. In the Orthodox Jewish world, whenever there is a *simcha,* or happy occasion, the doors are open to people who need money, whether for themselves or for others.

But finally, one of my fellow guests at the table became annoyed. "I've been giving all evening to one *schnorrer* after another," he told a rabbi asking him for a donation. "Enough's enough!"

The rabbi looked at him in indignation. "What do you mean, enough's enough?" he shot back. "You should be grateful to me that I'm letting you give. Because of me you have the chance to do a great *mitzvah!*"

A *mitzvah* is a good deed. In the Zen Peacemaker Order, a good deed is an action that puts doubt in someone's head. Suddenly there's a question. And when there's a question, we're in the realm of unknowing.

Peacemakers who accompany us on the streets have to tell their friends. They risk rejection, anger, indifference. Most important, they wonder what it's all about. Their friends wonder, too. Everyone's paradigms get shifted around a little. All because we're asking for money.

Ultimately peacemakers discover that it's not

about rejection or acceptance—in fact, it's not about them. Asking for money is about giving someone an opportunity to do a *mitzvah,* a good deed. It's about offering them a meal. If they eat it, fine. If they don't, that's fine, too. The most we can do is offer.

When we go to the Bowery to bear witness to life on the streets, we're offering ourselves. Not blankets, not food, not clothes, just ourselves. We put away the things we identify with: watches, jewelry, money, credit cards. As a Zen priest I am usually clean-shaven with a bald head. I leave that identity behind me, too, and by the time we go out on the retreat my hair and beard have grown. We go with the clothes on our backs, nothing more. For the first street retreats I permitted people to carry two dollars a day for emergency money. Now we carry no money.

That doesn't mean we've completely left our identities behind. All of us know that this is just for five days and that we'll return home, exhausted, to a hot bath, hot food, and a warm, clean bed. In the same way, you can't ever cook a meal entirely from scratch. Even if you buy all new ingredients you'll use your old kitchen tools, your old recipes, and most important, your old conditioning and training on how to cook, what makes a good main course, and how to set the table, among other things. So even though we don't shave and we carry no money, we take our thoughts and feelings with us, and for many of us those are of people with stable homes and stable lives.

But the streets have a funny way of working on people. When we begin our walk from Yonkers to the Bowery, our journey into the unknown, we still carry with us traces of our identities, our conditioning, our expectations, the images of who we are. In the succeeding days much of that will be stripped away. As our minds enter the unknown and we bear witness to life on the streets, Jim Morton's words become true. The unexpected—the street—becomes our teacher.

— 19 —

The Letten

We follow several rules during our street retreats. We always break into small packs, three or four participants per pack. Each pack goes its own way to find food, hang out with other people on the streets, and keep warm and dry. The members of each pack must stay together. The men are separated from the women because some food pantries serve only one gender and not the other. But we spend the nights together. We also try to get together twice a day for meditation and service at a place I designate ahead of time.

This meeting place is very important. During our first five street retreats we used to assemble at a crack park on the corner of Christie and Houston in lower Manhattan. People were shooting up all around us as we sat by a deserted basketball court. Before beginning our meditation sessions we always picked up some of the needles, vials, glass, and trash that littered the ground. Finally, around 1995, I went down to look at the park again before a street retreat and found that it was under construction. The neighborhood was becoming gentrified and the park was closed for renovation. I knew it wasn't going to be the same any longer, so we moved up to Tompkins Square Park in Alphabet City, close to the Bowery.

What are these places where we sit together, warming up in the sun some days, huddling together against the cold and the damp on others? Why am I drawn to sit there, meditate there, hold a service there?

During the early years I chose these places through intuition, without knowing exactly why. After visiting Auschwitz for the first time I realized that places of great suffering were also places of great healing. But the healing cannot arise until we bear witness to the suffering.

Most of us miss that. What we see are people sleeping on the concrete in the middle of the day, shooting up, peeing in the open because they have no bathroom, or else gathered around a fire in an iron can with bottles in paper bags. What we see is garbage on the ground and graffiti on the walls. We see a place of suffering and chaos, and we want to get away. But in trying to leave the suffering behind, we never see the possibilities for healing. Each of these places has tremendous healing energy—not just for those who live there, but also for those of us who visit and bear witness.

In May 1993, I participated in an interfaith conference just outside Zurich, Switzerland. The Jesuit who organized that conference, Father Niklaus Brantschen, had once come with us on the streets in New York City. He invited me to the conference, and while I was there he told me about the famous Zurich drug park called the Letten. A short while before, the Zurich authorities, realizing the extent of drug use in the city, had begun an experiment. They'd sectioned off a large embankment the size of a football field just outside the very center of town, within easy walking distance of the train station, and allowed the purchase, sale, and use of drugs to take place there. Their rationale was that addicts should have a safe place in which they could buy and use drugs instead of having to do it illegally, often engaging in criminal or dangerous activities to feed their habits. Safe needles would be given out to prevent the spread of disease. And by bringing addicts out in public it was hoped they would be more accessible to social workers and drug counselors.

Unfortunately, while the Swiss addicts did indeed congregate at the Letten, other addicts did, too. Dealers and users came to the Letten from all over the world, including Southeast Asia and South America, to take advantage of this new legal drug market.

After the conference I was taken to see the Letten. What I saw there I don't think I'll forget in my entire life.

The Letten was on a low embankment by the railroad tracks, on both sides of the river feeding into Lake Zurich. From one end to the other people were shooting up heroin, sniffing cocaine, using every conceivable drug in the world. We began to make our way through the Letten, and there were thousands of people there. Some were completely stoned, some were hallucinating. They were alone, in couples, or in small groups exchanging big stashes of cash for drugs. The area was so packed with humanity that at times we had to push our way through. Some of the people were sprawled on the ground, totally oblivious to us as we made our way through the park. Imagine an open food market, selling every food from around the world, packed with food growers, vendors, buyers, retailers, wholesalers, and people eating whatever they bought right at the scene. Now imagine that same market, only with drugs instead of food, and you'll get a tiny glimpse of what the Letten in Zurich looked like that Sunday afternoon.

We were told that sixteen thousand needles were being given away each day at the Letten. We trod them underfoot with each step we took, walking around thousands of addicts lying in a stupor on the grass or bathing or washing in the river, all ignoring us completely. Even the dealers ignored us as they exchanged piles of currency in all denominations. And as I looked up I saw Swiss policemen high over the embankment monitoring the scene.

I felt as though I were in a scene from Dante's *Inferno*. Once again, I was surrounded by hungry ghosts. Their cries, most of them silent, were all around me, clamoring, wanting, needing, always hungry. The drug addicts were like sheep herded inside an enclosure, away from the beautiful streets of the city, far from the eyes of the rest of society. The dealers carried guns to protect their money, their faces full of greed for the profits they might make. And just a short distance away was Zurich's Bahnhofstrasse, one of Europe's most expensive shopping streets, full of banks laundering the dealers' cash for later use and distribution. The Letten was full of greed, anger, and ignorance. It was also a living metaphor of a society in denial, blaming those who were suffering, aiding and abetting the perpetrators, thriving financially on the proceeds from that suffering, taking no responsibility, simply looking away.

Then and there I knew I had to come back and sit in the Letten for several days, surrounded by the vials, needles, matches, and white powder, beneath the indifferent gaze of the Swiss policemen protecting society from contact with its own disease, its own pain. I felt a powerful urge to sit right in the middle of it all.

But a month before my next visit to Zurich I was informed by Niklaus that the Letten had been closed. The Zurich authorities had decided they'd had enough. Their experiment hadn't worked out. They hadn't counted on so many foreigners arriving by train at the city terminal and walking straight to the Letten. And the horrible scene offended their sensibilities. So one day, without any warning, the policemen came down and threw all the people out of the Letten, leaving it empty and wasted.

Even then it wasn't over. Drug users continued to be drawn to the Letten as if to a magnet, even though drug deals were no longer permitted there. The police fenced the area completely so that no one could go inside.

I, too, was drawn to the Letten. I had never seen so much human devastation so densely packed in an enclosed area. To this day I regret that I was never able to sit for several days in the middle of all that suffering.

People have asked me, "What would have happened had you sat in the Letten for days, even weeks? Do you think somebody would have stopped using? Do you think somebody would have stopped selling drugs because you sat there?"

My answer is that I don't know. When you bear witness, you go with no preconceived notions about what you'll see and what will happen. I wanted to sit there and find out. Bearing witness means to have a relationship. I wanted to have a relationship with the Letten and all its inhabitants, as I subsequently wished

to have a relationship with Auschwitz and all its inhabitants, as I try to do with the places where we sit during street retreats and all their inhabitants. Out of
bearing witness, out of the relationship, a healing arises.
In what form, through what activity or event, through
what person, I have no idea. But I knew for certain that
healing would arise in the Letten. Of itself, fruit would
be born.

Since the Letten was no longer available we did
a street retreat in another park in Zurich, in
Beckeranlage, behind Helvetiaplatz. To the eyes of
someone from New York who'd spent time on the
streets of New York City and Yonkers, the Zurich park
looked different at first glimpse. The grass was cut.
Mothers wheeled their children through the park during the day. There was a bandstand for concerts. There
was no trash on the ground. But if you looked more
closely you noticed groups of young people sitting
together on the grass, sharing drugs. A young woman
went into convulsions not ten feet away from where we
sat for our evening meditation.

As night neared we brought plastic and cardboard boxes from the surrounding streets. We spent the
night on the wooden steps of the bandstand alongside
men who were regulars at the park, their liquor bottles
at arm's length. The park got very empty except for the
frequent headlights of the police cars looking us over
very carefully as they drove by. Our group included
Jesuits and nuns, but those beams searched us as thor-
oughly as they did the others. In the middle of the
night one of the homeless men began to mutter angrily
that we should leave, that on account of us the police
would come and throw everyone out. But his friend

told him we were good people, and one of our party, a young Jesuit, reminded him that, after all, the parks are for everyone.

At two in the morning I gave up on the prospect of sleeping in the cold. Accompanying me on that street retreat was my student Eve Marko. She was one of those who had strongly objected to my street retreats when I first went out in 1991. The Zurich retreat was her first time on the streets with me. In the early hours that morning she and I walked up and down the neighborhood surrounding the park. This was the red-light district of Zurich. As we passed, windows opened and women looked out, waiting for customers. We were told that many Russian women had come to Zurich eager to make a living out of prostitution. Their pimps waited at the corners, scrutinizing us carefully as we came near, searching for a hint of our intentions.

Annual street retreats now take place each May at the Beckeranlage park in Zurich. In addition, a small group meditates there every week. The park draws them in the way the Letten drew me, in the same way I feel a sense of home when I approach Tompkins Square Park in New York City. In fact, one of the group members who works in the area has told me that she visits the park almost every day. She says she can't help it.

From year to year we see our New York park change. At times we have not been permitted to sit on the grass at Tompkins Square because it's been replanted. There are more guards now, including two who stand outside the bathrooms to check whoever goes in and to lock the bathrooms at five P.M. sharp.

There are no doors to the stalls in the bathrooms. The police patrol constantly. While there, we get to know the regulars, the men who play chess, and the King and Queen of Punk who panhandle at the corner accompanied by their dog. If too many changes happen to Tompkins Square Park and it no longer feels the same to me, like the park at the corner of Christie and Houston, I will probably find a new place in which to sit, meditate, and generally hang out.

What I'm looking for is a certain energy, the energy of bearing witness. In Auschwitz, in the Letten, and in shabby city parks, people lose their layers and pretensions. They lose their knowing. That's when they start to see things at ground level and to bear witness.

And what exactly do we do in these parks? Twice a day, in the morning and in the late afternoon, we do a meditation for half an hour, seated on the grass or on concrete benches, wherever we're permitted. We also do a Buddhist service that has been the service of the Zen Community of New York for many years, reflecting its—and my—particular ministry. It says, in part:

"Raising the Mind of Compassion, the Supreme Meal is offered to all the hungry spirits throughout space and time, filling the smallest particle to the largest space. All you hungry spirits in the Ten Directions, please gather here. Sharing your distress, I offer you this food, hoping it will resolve your thirsts and hungers."

Where We Eat

We eat in food pantries. We eat in churches, missions, and mosques. We panhandle for coffee, tea, and even fresh fruit at delis and restaurants. We get bologna-and-cheese sandwiches for breakfast from the Franciscan brothers on West Thirty-first Street.

I love coffee. I have always been a coffee drinker; I drink it all day, including during the evening. I joke that I need a strong cup of coffee at night in order to fall asleep. But if you drink coffee you need to pee. After my first street retreat I learned to avoid coffee on the streets. Which is just as well, because getting coffee is not easy. Many places that give out sandwiches won't give out coffee. You can't wrap hot cups of coffee in plastic, put them in a box hours ahead of time, and then give them out. You need to make the coffee in quantity, and you need to keep it hot.

I remember panhandling for coffee on our first street retreat. It happened the night we slept in cardboard boxes on the streets of Chinatown. It was cold and it was raining. In fact, it rained every day of that retreat. We found boxes and plastic and laid them all out. The rest of the group was ready to call it a day, but I needed my fix, my evening cup of coffee. So I started panhandling for money. I'd already been told that it wasn't easy to panhandle in Chinatown. After a long, long time someone finally gave me a quarter. I had kept the Styrofoam cup I'd used at the Bowery Mission, where we'd eaten dinner, so armed with the quarter and the Styrofoam cup I started panhandling for coffee. None of the places in Chinatown would give me any.

Finally I entered a basement coffee shop, several steps down from street level. I approached the counter and said to the man, "I have a cup and I have a quarter. Can I get some coffee?"

The man looked behind him at somebody else, obviously the boss. The boss looked back at me. I was grungy and wet from the rain outside. "Yeah, give it to him," the boss said.

The man poured coffee into my Styrofoam cup while I put my quarter on the counter. I felt very happy. This was the first time I'd panhandled on the streets, and finally, after a couple of hours, I had my cup of coffee. I went outside and slipped on the wet steps going up to the street. The cup fell from my hands and the hot coffee spilled all over me.

Just because we're on the streets doesn't mean that we lose our personalities or our distinct ways of doing things. Our styles, our idiosyncrasies, our particular ways of getting food and surviving shine through even though we all wear ragged street clothes with no money in our pockets. One of the people who has come with me on the streets panhandles by playing his shakuhachi flute for coins. Claude Thomas, with his lengthy experience of recovery programs, goes from one meeting to another looking for free coffee and donuts.

On one of our street retreats we heard from a

homeless man living in a shantytown under the Manhattan Bridge that he never eats in food pantries because he doesn't like their food. Instead he goes to the restaurants down by Fulton Street and takes the leftovers off the tables. After hearing this we all made our way south to Fulton Street. There we found a restaurant,—South Sea,—that served pizza, salad, and pasta. Sure enough, people left the tables heaped with leftovers. One of the retreat participants was the CEO of a record company. While the rest of us watched, he took out a plastic bag, hurried to the empty tables, and collected the scraps and leftovers in the big bag. The customers were sure Tommy was a waiter. He managed to collect quite a bit before the restaurant finally threw him out.

Tommy was also the best collector of cans in our entire group. He collected the biggest and best cardboard boxes for the night. His entrepreneurial skills shone. It didn't matter that he was on the streets with no money in his pockets, he made every situation a success.

From the beginning we were told by friends who'd lived on the streets that we would find a lot of food. Over the years I've found that to be almost always true. So although we never take a bed needed by a homeless person, we eat whenever we can; food pantries are glad to share their food with us. The only things we miss on the streets are fresh vegetables and fruit—and sometimes we find those, too.

I also noticed from the beginning that the food pantries and missions have their own styles of giving food, just like people. So on every street retreat I make it a habit to visit different places for our meals so that the people with me can see the many different ways of giving that exist on the streets.

The Franciscan monks wear their habits as they stand outside their mission, around the corner from Macy's and Herald Square, providing bologna-and-cheese sandwiches. Several food pantries near the Bowery are run by the Catholic Worker, one serving only women and one serving both men and women. The latter serves great soup and bread accompanied by heavy rock and rap music on a boom box. The women in our group have told us that it's quieter in the other pantry, housed in the building where Dorothy Day, founder of the Catholic Worker, lived and died, and that staff members sit at the small tables and have friendly chats with whoever comes in. They have even been invited to take showers on certain days of the week. The pantry also has a small secondhand clothing outlet where you can look for a hat or a scarf, maybe even an extra sweater, against the cold.

Then there's the Bowery Mission, where we pray before we eat. The Bowery Mission feeds hundreds of people every day, and a Baptist service before dinner is compulsory. Singers, preachers, and small youth groups, attended by an organ, guitars, and other musical instruments, come from all over the country to preach at the Bowery Mission. Some people complain about having to go through preaching and a service before they're fed. I have learned many things from my work in Yonkers and from living on the streets. One is that drugs are the religion of the streets. For a fleeting moment they seem to create a transformation out of misery and suffering. After a couple of drinks or a couple of hits people don't notice that they're hungry, that they've lost their families, and that they have nowhere to go. For a brief time they feel important, wanted, and out of pain. Of course, when they come back down they feel in even greater pain than before, and they need an even bigger fix. People who are homeless and hooked on drugs and alcohol need to have a great faith that their lives will get better if they stop drinking or using. Faith in Christ or Allah can be that faith.

Of course, many of the people who come for the dinner fall asleep at the service. But at the end, when those present are asked to come forward and be saved, some come forward. If you step up to attest to your faith in Christ you are invited to stay at the mission, live there, work there, and finally make the move to a stable home and a job. And after the service, whether you've been saved or not, you're served a hearty meal.

I heard about the Bowery Mission prior to our very first street retreat from Oscar, one of the tenants at the Greyston Family Inn apartments. He spoke warmly of the two years he'd spent there before coming up to Greyston. In particular, he told me to find Brother James, who'd been with him at the mission and was now on staff. What he didn't tell me was that he called Brother James himself to alert him that we were coming and to look out for our welfare.

We walked into the Bowery Mission, grizzled, wet, and hungry (that street retreat was the wettest retreat of all). After days of sleeplessness, rain, and cold, we thought we wouldn't stand out so much. In fact, I even asked everyone to go in singly and mix with the rest of the large group so that we wouldn't be conspicuous. But a young man came over to the poet Anne

Waldman, one of our group, and asked her who she was. She told him the truth. We were a group of activists living on the streets for a week. Brother James had found us.

A big, portly man, he talked to the group, describing the programs of the mission, which include housing and jobs, in addition to feeding hundreds of people every day. One day, as we were seated at the tables that would later hold dinner, he asked us if we wanted to hear his story. We did, so he told us.

Like many of the people there, he'd had many lives rolled into one. For years he was a drug user and dealer, making lots and lots of money. His life went up and then it went down, and finally, having lost everything, he ended up on the streets. He was not only homeless and moneyless, he was also angry. He was especially angry at white people. One night found him lying on a subway car seat, trying to get some sleep. It was two in the morning. Suddenly he was awakened by someone shaking his shoulder. He opened his eyes and looked up, ready to kill the man, probably a cop. But it wasn't a cop. It wasn't even a man. It was a woman.

"She looked just like you," he said to one of the white women in our group. "She was brave, too. She didn't know she was brave, but I knew she was brave to wake me up like that. 'Cause I was ready to kill. And you know what she said to me? You know what she said to this big, angry, unwashed, unshaven, smelly man, eyes bloodshot, clothes ragged—you know what she said to that man? She said, 'What's a man like you doing in a place like this?' That's what she said. That's what she said. I was so amazed I just sat there. At first I'd thought I was going to kill her for waking me up.

Instead I just sat there. And she gave me a card with the name of this place on it, Bowery Mission, and told me to go there. So I did. And I've been here ever since."

Not everybody in the Bowery Mission has a success story like Brother James or Oscar. The former says he's seen many people come and go. He's seen people stay clean for twenty years and then trip themselves up.

In 1991, during our first visit to the Bowery Mission, I also met Benny. Benny worked on staff and had contracted AIDS during his years of drug use. I'd rarely seen anyone more positive and upbeat than him. Every weekend he'd go up to Tompkins Square Park with the mission truck, bringing hot soup and tracts about Jesus Christ. He was thin and small and he was dying, and to the very end he kept on bringing food to the homeless men around the Bowery, razzing them, telling them to come to the mission and that Jesus Christ was his Savior. It was Benny who'd brought Oscar to the mission two years before, and even after Oscar came up to live at Greyston, he'd go down to visit with Benny and help him in his work. Benny died in 1995.

We learned that the Bowery Mission used to be a morgue.

"They used to come in dead and leave dead," they say. "Now some come in dead and leave alive."

— 21 —

Aimless Meandering

We have a schedule for street retreats in the same way that we have a schedule for any other retreat. The difference is that it's impossible to stick to it.

For instance, the schedule calls for us to meet in Tompkins Square Park twice a day for service and meditation. That way the various packs all come together to check in and talk about their experiences. Also, in case anyone gets lost they know where to find us. But the streets have their own schedule. Rumor might have it that a great meat loaf lunch is being served someplace at noon. When we get there we find it's two hours later. Or we run into a Passion play on Avenue B on Good Friday. By the time it's over we're a couple of hours late for our gathering at the park.

But the schedule remains a critical part of the retreat. It gives us some framework, a basic structure to which we can return when the day's events permit.

We also walk a lot. And walking, particularly after only a few hours of sleep at night, often takes longer than we think. On the schedule I call it "aimless meandering." Many of us who go on the streets lead very hectic, structured lives, with every hour accounted for. On the streets we all meander aimlessly, looking at everything from street level. We notice things we don't usually have time to notice. We take a good look at the bodegas around the block, the graffiti on the walls, buildings that are crumbling and those that are being gentrified, people sitting on a stoop, the condition of the pavement, the school yards and the parks, the trash that collects at corners. We talk to people. We ask them how they're doing. We ask them where there's a good place to get some food. We start to see more and more ingredients. We start to bear witness.

We walk up Eighth Avenue from Penn Station just before dawn after being kicked out of the waiting area by the police, passing person after person, building after building, one blinking traffic light after another, no watches on our wrists, no appointment to keep, walking everywhere but arriving nowhere. It's just the cold mist before dawn, the hot air coming out of the subway vents in the pavement, the trucks making very early deliveries. We're just walking, just meandering, not doing much of anything.

When I go on the streets I feel as if I've put behind me all the details and concerns of my daily life. I feel lighter on my feet and in my heart. Life is simple. When it rains we try to find a dry spot; if we don't, we get wet. When it's cold we try to find a warm spot; if we don't, we're cold. If we're tired, we're just tired. If we're hungry, we're just hungry. It's no big deal.

Most people who've joined me feel the same way. Whether they're corporate executives or busy professionals, they say they feel freer on the streets at a street retreat than they've felt for years. Ironically, back home and in the office people think they're crazy. But on the streets, with no money or credit cards in their pockets, just the clothes on their backs, they're happy.

In fact, it's the very lack that scares their friends—the lack of identification, funds, extra clothes and shoes, a home, protection—that gives them this taste of simplicity, freedom, and even joy. For what they've also discovered is that out on the streets they have everything they need.

We can find everything we need on the streets if we can make shifts in our paradigms. If we want to find a place to sleep and we're looking for warm, comfortable beds, we won't find them. But when we start looking for anything that might help us sleep we find cardboard boxes, plastic, discarded blankets and coats, even an old fur jacket. We find that newspapers stuffed in shoes are good insulation against the cold. This process is a reflection of just how quickly, and to what extent, we can drop our notions, our knowing.

When Eve accompanied me on the Zurich street retreat—her first time on the streets—she didn't want to pick up cardboard and plastic to sleep in because they were dirty. It wasn't her usual way of preparing for bed. After just one night without them she understood why they were necessary and then she gathered them with enthusiasm. At that same retreat there was a man who had brought with him an entire backpack with a fancy sleeping bag. This was against our rules, but he came with us nevertheless, carrying it with him all day. Naturally, this limited his ability to meander aimlessly. At night he was warm and comfortable, but he defeated the purpose of going on the streets, which is to examine the ingredients at hand and make a meal out of them. He brought his own ingredients from home. If instead he'd gone out fearlessly, he'd have discovered that the streets had everything he needed.

One of my students from Long Island once came on the streets with me. He had forgotten his belt at home, so he had trouble keeping his pants up, which got in the way of his aimless meandering. One of the women with us knew how to sew. She found a potato sack on the streets. While riding the subway that night, going from one end of the city to the other in order to stay warm, she loosened the threads of the sack and braided them together to make him a belt. It served the purpose beautifully.

Of course, much of the time we have a destination or a purpose to our walking. You can spend all day doing nothing but going from a meal to a bathroom, to Tompkins Park, to the next meal, to a bathroom, to Tompkins Park once again, to a deli to see if they'll give you a cup of coffee, to a bathroom, to the next meal, to find a place to sleep, to find plastic and cardboard. You begin to understand why street people walk as much as they do. And after spending sleepless nights at Penn Station, on subways, in Central Park, or on the pavements, you also understand why so many of them sleep during the day. They can't get much sleep during the night because it's cold and they get chased away by the cops. We also slept during the day on the ground and on the benches in the park, snoozing under the warm sun while the guards left us alone.

Street retreats bring us smack against life in all its immediacy. Regular retreats do the same thing— but, in my experience, not as dramatically as street retreats. On the streets, issues of eating, peeing, defecating, and sleeping are raw and right in front of your face. As are issues of rejection. After just one day on the street people begin to reject you, to deny your existence. When you walk into a restaurant they won't serve you, they won't even let you in. When you ask if you can use the bathroom they say no. People walk away from you because they don't like the way you smell or look.

If you truly experience this you will never avoid street people again, these people that are you. You won't avoid the drug addicts, the cops, the panhandlers, the hustlers and the pimps, their johns, the bulges under the blankets in the doorways, the men at the counters who pour you a cup of coffee, those who don't, the veterans sitting on the sidewalks in their fatigues, the people with an open hand, giving and receiving, and the people with the hand shut tight, almost making a fist. Why? Because you've listened, and all these people are you.

— 22 —

The Abundance of
the Streets

One of the biggest lessons I have learned from our street retreats is about the abundance of the streets. When we go with nothing but the clothes on our backs, we're opening up, letting go of our usual concepts. And when we do that, we find that the streets just give and give and give endlessly.

I could write a book about nothing but the generosity of the streets and what happens when we're ready to ask and receive. During each retreat I insist that people panhandle for what they want. Even when I still permitted participants to carry two dollars a day, this money was meant to be used only for emergencies. So one afternoon in Tompkins Square Park, when I saw Arnie, one of my students, with a cup of tea, I asked him how he got it.

"I bought it from the man at the small deli on the corner," he told me.

This wasn't good. By using his emergency money to buy a cup of tea, Arnie had essentially checked out of the streets and gone back to his usual way of doing things—namely, buying what he needed.

"Arnie, give me your money," I said. "All of it." I took away not just his allotment for that day but the money for the rest of the retreat, ten dollars in all.

"From now on," I told him, "when you want tea, you ask for it."

Arnie went back to the deli on the corner with his cup and the used teabag and asked for a refill of hot water. They gave it to him. He panhandled for cups of tea for the rest of the retreat. Sometimes he got them, sometimes he didn't. But he was no longer relying on money. He was living in the realm of giving and receiving, and learning a lesson about abundance.

Like most of us, Arnie was taught that nothing in life was free and that it's better not to ask for anything. We have great anxiety about what will happen if we lose our jobs, get sick, and get old. How will we live if we can't pay our bills? When we go on the streets and discover that what we need is right here, we develop more faith in life's basic goodness.

Much of the time we take our cups from coffee shop to coffee shop and encounter rejection, averted looks, denial. Mostly it's on account of how we look and smell. For most of the people who come with me on the streets, this is the first time this has ever happened to them, and it is probably the toughest part of the retreat. Almost nobody enjoys panhandling. They'd rather go without food or drink, as long as they don't have to ask. But if they don't ask, they won't receive.

Eve once walked with an empty Styrofoam cup in her hand from coffee shop to coffee shop around Tompkins Square Park, but wherever she went people said no. She was pretty discouraged when she finally went into a run-down store selling newspapers and candy, with two burners for coffee. She asked the man for a cup of coffee. He said no. She asked again, and he said no. Then she heard a man's voice next to her saying, "I'll buy her a cup." She turned to thank him, and as he put his hand into his pocket for the coins she noticed how he was dressed. His clothes were shabby and his shoes were torn. He wore no socks. But without another word he took out fifty cents and put the money on the counter.

Later she told me, "A poor man, probably somebody from the streets, bought me a cup of coffee. All the people with money whom I'd asked said no, but he said yes."

We insist on paying for things, staying separate and alienated from street life, because we're afraid of rejection. In fact, many of the people who come with me, faced with a lack of money, prefer to live without rather than risk a turn-down. They're actually more comfortable with isolation and deprivation than with asking and receiving. I have to push them to ask.

There are days when the streets shower us with gifts. We are standing on line in front of the Franciscan mission, waiting patiently for our breakfast sandwiches. At seven o'clock a bakery truck pulls over. Its doors open. Immediately several men on line, clearly accustomed to this routine, run over and unload boxes full of wedge rolls, fresh and delicious. They unpack the boxes and go up and down the line, handing out the rolls to all of us. I have no idea which bakery sends over those fresh rolls, but I'm glad it does.

We miss lunch one day at the food pantry and arrive hungry at Tompkins Square Park. It's a long wait till dinner. Suddenly someone comes by to say that organic vegetarian food is being served on the other side of the park. Organic vegetarian food in Tompkins Park? We walk over. Sure enough, a few young men are ladling soup, mashed potatoes, and vegetable salad from large plastic containers. They're squatters living in some of the condemned buildings in the neighborhood, they tell us, and they've been serving three lunches a week every week for the last three years in the park. They also have one-day-old pastries, so for dessert we eat cheese Danishes and fruit muffins. They tell us where and when they cook and invite us to help whenever we're around.

There's a Buddhist sutra, or teaching, we often recite during a morning service. One of its verses says: "When you don't see the Way, you don't see it even as you walk on it." What is this Way? What is the Way of the streets? Opening the hand, letting go of our things, letting go of our knowing, and bearing witness to giving and receiving, is the Way.

The more we empty ourselves, the fuller our lives become. The irony is that most people acquire more and more things all the time, trying to realize that fullness, only to discover instead how empty their lives are!

An African man who works with homeless people and has accompanied me on the streets has told me that in his African village it was customary for boys to leave the village and become homeless for eighteen months as a step into adulthood. "When people go on the street with you," he said, "they learn something from it. But I work with people who live for years on the streets and they don't learn anything. They are destroyed by the streets, instead of finding life on the streets. Why is that?"

Eve, remembering her poor childhood, was upset when I first started going on the streets. "You have no idea what it means to be poor," she told me. "Street retreats are condescending and insensitive." When she finally began joining us, she learned that whatever you need is right there. She had not learned this as a girl growing up in a poor family.

The abundance of life is not visible to those who have much or to those who have little. If you have a great deal you think that your wealth lies in your money in the bank, your home, your job, your pension. If you have little you believe you'll achieve wealth if you get money in the bank, a home, a job, a pension. In both cases, only if you let go of your ideas will you realize that right in front of you is everything you need.

Finally, this is what happened to us on the streets on the morning of Maundy Thursday during Holy Week of 1996. Upon leaving St. Mark's Church in the East Village, where we'd been permitted to spend the rainy night, I found one of my students and peacemaker priests, Michael O'Keefe, reading the *New York Times*.

"Where did you get the paper?" I asked Michael.

"The vendor up the street," he said. "I wanted to get the paper when I saw the headlines. Ron Brown was killed in a plane crash over Yugoslavia."

"Did you ask him to give it to you, Michael?"

"No," Michael said, "I paid for it."

I reminded him that the two dollars he had in his pocket was for emergencies only, certainly not to buy a paper. "Give me your money," I told him.

Michael forked over his entire ten-dollar weekly allotment, complaining, "I just wanted to get the paper this one time. I wanted to read about Ron Brown."

As we were talking a man came down the block

toward us carrying a number of copies of the *New York Times*. He came to a stop right in front of Michael. "You want a paper?" he asked. "You can have it for a quarter."

Michael didn't say anything for about ten seconds. Then he said, quite truthfully, "I don't have a quarter."

The man then asked the rest of us if we wanted a paper for a quarter and we all shook our heads. He muttered under his breath and then proceeded down the block. Michael looked at me. Before he could say anything, we heard steps again. The man was coming back.

"What the hell, nobody's buying any, you can have them for nothing," he said, dropping the papers on the bench and walking away.

After that no more money was allowed on street retreats. Not even for emergencies.

— 23 —

Holy Week

I have always loved the world of interfaith encounters and celebrations. As a Jew who became a Zen Buddhist priest and teacher, I already embodied two very different religious traditions. And from my earliest days as a Zen teacher in New York I was deeply interested in how each religious tradition manifests the oneness of life, the oneness of God. I have also had students of Zen who are Catholic nuns and priests, Sufi sheiks, and rabbis, and have empowered some of them as Zen teachers in my lineage.

In the early years of the Zen Community of New York, when we had a large retreat center, we held Passover seders, Sabbath celebrations, and Catholic masses. The Quakers in our neighborhood held their meetings at our center. Since one of my earliest students was Lex Hixon, a Sufi sheik, it was common for Zen students to go down to his New York City mosque on Thursday nights for the weekly *zikr.* I consider Reb Zalman Schachter-Shalomi, perhaps the key figure in the modern Jewish Revival movement, and Jim Morton, who served as dean of the Cathedral of St. John the Divine for twenty-five years, two of my closest friends and also as spiritual mentors. They have

inspired me through many years of joint services, celebrations, events, talks, and workshops.

I believe that an appreciation of the differences
among religious traditions, as well as the spirituality
they have in common, is essential to healing our world
and putting an end to its conflicts, many of which take
place in the name of religious ideology. But for now I
wish to talk about going on the streets during Holy
Week, the week of Easter, the week of Passover, one of
the saddest and most joyous times of the year.

Since 1991, our Holy Week street retreat has
included witnessing different religious celebrations and
services that take place during that week all around the
city. I go on the streets at other times of the year, too,
and each occasion is special in its own way, but the
streets feel different during Holy Week. The remembrance and caring that spring to life during that
time are unmistakable and unforgettable.

We ended our first street retreat in 1991 on the
night before Easter with both a Passover seder and a
Catholic mass at City Hall Park. It had poured that
whole week, and it poured that night, too. We'd told
people on the streets about these celebrations, but we
thought nobody would come on account of the
weather. As the time neared, street people began to
come into the park. They emerged from the bushes and
came up the paths through the downpour. We were
about a hundred people altogether.

The rain came down in torrents. I looked up at
City Hall. The steps led to a covered verandah where
we could stay dry. A guard stood at the top of the steps.
I went up. "We're holding a Passover seder and a
Catholic mass," I explained to him. "All these people

came to participate, including a rabbi and a priest. Can we do this here?" He, too, was wet. He said it was fine with him but he had to check with his boss, who was inside. He went inside, then came out. His boss had said no. So we held our celebrations in the rain.

Everyone waited patiently as Don Singer passed out matzos and bitter herbs with grape juice and told the story of liberation from slavery, the long journey from addiction to freedom. He broke the matzo and spoke about a broken heart. Only a broken heart is a healing heart, Don said.

Members of the Zen Community of New York brought hot chicken soup with matzo balls. They also brought cookies from the Greyston Bakery. While Don continued to talk about Passover, I sat next to two men who'd come to join us. One turned to the other. "So when's he going to give us food?" he asked. And I heard the other reply, "You know, sometimes you have to wait for the good things."

When Don finished the seder, Father Robert Kennedy, a Jesuit and also a Zen teacher, conducted a mass under a broken umbrella held by a Buddhist. "The bread we are eating, the body of Christ, was broken on the cross to feed everyone," he told us all. Many came up to his small table to receive communion.

That was the last time we had food sent down from Yonkers as part of a street retreat. After that I insisted that we find the food on the streets, even for Passover. But the tradition of religious celebrations during Holy Week continued. Sometimes we hosted those celebrations, at other times we joined in as guests.

For me, interfaith celebrations are evidence of the abundance of life. To give you a feel for what I mean, let me describe the 1996 Holy Week street retreat.

We spent our first night sleeping—or trying to sleep—in Central Park. It was so cold that at about four A.M. we gave up and began to walk downtown, stopping for breakfast at the Franciscan mission on West Thirty-first Street en route to our hangout at Tompkins Square Park. We were tired, and it didn't help when we heard that it was going to rain that night, the first night of Passover. Walking past St. Mark's Church in the East Village, I ran into its rector, Lloyd Casson. Notwithstanding the smell of my clothes after a night in the park, Lloyd gave me a hug. I knew Lloyd from when he'd served as rector of Trinity Church, and before that as assistant dean at the Cathedral of St. John the Divine. When he heard that we would be in the area, Lloyd suggested we come to the Tenebrae service at St. Mark's after our Passover seder and then spend the night in the church.

Rabbi Don had flown in from California to join us for Passover on the streets, but he'd disappeared in the middle of our night in Central Park. For purposes of the seder, we begged for food in the Jewish restaurants on Second Avenue and in Spanish bodegas by Tompkins Square. One retreat participant, a Swiss woman, was given twenty dollars by the Franciscans when she attended their mass that morning before breakfast. Suddenly, as we began to give up hope, Don appeared in Tompkins Square Park. He explained that he'd been so cold during the night that he'd gone into the subway to keep warm. After riding the trains all night he'd visited a few Jewish temples, asking them for food for our seder. He arrived with bottles of kosher grape juice and gefilte fish. Using the money the Franciscans had given us, we bought more food and then, at nightfall, held a seder at Tompkins Park.

We sat around two picnic tables in an enclosure behind the park's rest rooms. We invited the park regulars to join us, including the King and Queen of Punk, accompanied by their dog. Again Don passed around matzos, bitter herbs, and grape juice, and we talked about leaving Egypt, the land of bondage, addictions, and delusions, and arriving in the Promised Land. We told the story of slavery and the story of freedom, we sang and danced, Don leading us around the tables. Finally we shared the food we'd gathered, and when the seder was over we walked to St. Mark's Church.

We found ourselves in the middle of the Tenebrae service. St. Mark's Church was designed for performances, so there are no pews, only an altar in front and risers on the sides. Chairs were brought out, candles were dimmed, and the church was dark at the end of this sad service about the Passion of Christ.

At the conclusion, Lloyd Casson told his president that the strange-looking group sitting in the back, with musty smells and grizzled faces, would be spending the night at the church. I could see some frenzied whispering going on. I walked over to Lloyd and said that we would be happy to camp outside, on the grounds of the church. But Lloyd was adamant. So we sat in the back along with a few of St. Mark's parishioners and introduced ourselves. We told them about spending the previous night in Central Park and about having just come from a seder in Tompkins Square Park. I talked a little about our annual street retreats. It didn't take long for the president of St. Mark's to change his mind and give us permission to stay. So that night we slept on the risers. The church was warm and dry, and the candles still burned from the service as we fell asleep. When we awoke we went into the vestry. There we found the president of the church, who had spent the night in the church along with us, busy making us a pot of coffee.

After the retreat I spoke to Lloyd, who told me what a difference that evening had made to his church. St. Mark's had had a long history of activism in the local community, but this had lapsed through the years. The church was in the process of reconsidering these priorities when we had walked in, tired and cold, and asked if we could spend the rainy night inside the church. Its directors were inspired, and they renewed their commitment to social action.

It was now Maundy Thursday, a day of divine mysteries. At noon a friend arrived in the park, bringing large quantities of Passover food for us. This was against the rules, but as soon as she spread out the food, people gathered from all over the park. In fact, the food went so fast that most of us had no chance to eat at all. Then a man came and invited us to lunch at St. Brigitte's Church, on the east side of the park.

Off we went to the basement of the church, where a huge meal had been prepared by the parishioners, who also showed us to our table and waited on us. After the meal, they ushered us to a long table in the corner piled high with home-baked cakes, pies, and cookies. The children of the church had prepared cards wishing us a Happy Easter.

After we had eaten they asked us if we would

like to have our feet washed. They took us behind a partition to a row of chairs and sat us down among other street people. I hesitated. My feet had painful, ugly blisters from our seventeen-mile walk from Yonkers to Tompkins Square just two days before. But one woman crouched in front of me and helped me take my shoes and socks off. She examined the blisters. They had punctured and were very red. Gently she dipped my feet into a basin of hot water. Then she massaged my feet.

"Why are you doing this?" I asked her.

"I am doing this because Jesus Christ did," the woman said, her manicured fingers running very gently over my sore feet. "He washed the feet of his disciples even though he was the Son of God, and that is why I do it, too."

She put special salve on my blisters. She also gave me a new pair of white socks.

The sun shone that afternoon, beautiful and warm as we sat undisturbed on the benches of Tompkins Square Park. We did our own Buddhist service, inviting all the hungry ghosts to partake with us in the Supreme Meal. And when that was over we began to make our way even farther downtown, toward the Masjid el-Farah. Its former sheik, my student and Zen teacher Lex Nur Hixon, had died of cancer six months earlier. His successor, Sheik Fariha, had invited us to participate in their weekly *zikr*.

It was twilight, and we were walking down one of the narrow streets of the financial district when we passed a synagogue I'd never seen before. It was brand-new, with a modern design. As we paused to admire it a man wearing a yarmulke came out. He looked at our showerless, unshaven group without the slightest curiosity and asked, "Are any of you Jews?"

As a matter of fact, we told him, about four of us were Jews. We even had a rabbi with us.

"Good," he announced. "We need your help to make a minyan."

A minyan is a quorum of ten men needed for Orthodox Jewish services. We went inside. The men were separated from the women, each gender sitting in a separate section. It was the second evening of Passover, and the Hebrew service went quickly. The rabbi spoke about the Passover temple sacrifices more than two thousand years ago, then led another short service. At the end he came over to us, shook our hands, thanked us, and out we went. Three blocks down, around the corner, was the Masjid el-Farah.

There we were greeted warmly by Sheik Fariha, an old friend, along with her husband, Sheik Hydar, and a large group of Sufis. They welcomed us to the second floor of the mosque, where we sat together around long, low tables holding large plates of oriental spiced chicken and rice, cheese, salads, and fresh fruit. Their joyful hospitality reminded me of Lex, who gave big hugs to every person who entered the mosque, regardless of his or her religion, with arms that seemed long enough to embrace all the people of the world. We described the evenings spent in Central Park and in St. Mark's Church. Don Singer spoke about the meaning of Passover. The poet Robert Bly joined the gathering and offered a poem. We sang "*La-illaha-il-allah* [There Is No God but Allah]."

Finally we went down to the mosque. Again,

men and women were separated, with the women covering their hair. In a place of no images a service was held, and we made many bows. And then the *zikr* began. *Zikr* means *remembrance*. Forming a circle within a circle, we whirled around, turning our faces from side to side, saying the name of Allah again and again, losing ourselves in His praise. Hour after hour we did this, calling on the divine names, forming circle after circle of ecstasy. The Sufis sang, the instruments played, we turned and whirled and danced. Rumi, the great Sufi poet and mystic, had written:

> In love with him, my soul
> Lives the subtlest of passions,
> Lives like a gypsy.
> Each day a different house,
> Each night under the stars.

During those five days we were abiding nowhere yet we were everywhere, drunk on the passion of God, Christ, Yahweh, and Allah. Wherever we went we were given food, shelter, friendship, and love. At every place we were greeted like long-lost children.

The following day, cold and rainy, was Good Friday. After a breakfast of green pea soup and bread at the Catholic Worker food pantry, we went back to St. Brigitte's to follow the annual Passion play. It began inside the church. A young Hispanic with long black hair, dressed in a simple white robe and sandals, was Christ. Roman soldiers mocked and whipped him, and finally hoisted a big cross onto his back. With Christ and the priest leading the way, a procession left the church, going around the Bowery, to stop at the

Stations of the Cross. It began to snow, and soon I could see Christ's sandals slipping on the wet, white pavement, his legs and feet red from the cold. But he carried the cross north on Avenue B, followed by the church's parishioners and us.

The snow turned to sleet and came down hard. We stopped at each Station of the Cross: a house that was a known hangout for drug dealers, a building where a shootout had taken place with the police, a house of prostitution, an abandoned tenement. We mingled with the people in the procession who struggled every day to build a life in that neighborhood for their families. We stopped at places of drugs, murder, squatting, homelessness, abuse, violence, and squalor, singing devoutly in English and Spanish, asking for forgiveness. Christ's mother approached him, wishing to cradle him in her arms. He spoke with the women of Jerusalem, who were none other than the women of Avenue B. He was stripped, whipped, scourged, frozen, humiliated, friendless. And when we returned to the church he was crucified. One of the retreat participants had left the street retreat the night before, then rejoined us at Tompkins Square Park after a change of heart. Now he wept and wept.

We finished our retreat at the Cathedral of St. John the Divine with a candlelight mass on the eve of Easter. Jim Morton knew we were coming and had saved us special seats, but that didn't prevent many of us from dozing off during the dark, somber service. We all awoke when suddenly the lights of the cathedral blazed on and the organ and choir began to sing loudly and joyfully that Christ, once again, had risen.

These were some of the events of our retreat in

Holy Week, 1996. Other things happened that week, too: a sleepless night at Penn Station, two people with such badly blistered feet that they had to leave us. One of the participants who'd served as my personal assistant, a talented musician with a history of drug use, went back to using that week. He'd fallen back on old habits several times in the past, and it wasn't even clear that he would participate in the retreat. In the end he pleaded with me to let him come. I did. On the eve of Maundy Thursday, as we lay on the risers of St. Mark's Church, he played melody after melody on the organ, lullabying us all to sleep. But the following day he disappeared. Someone else told me he'd gone to see a dealer. I didn't see him for a long, long time after that.

His story, too, is part of our Holy Week street retreat. The retreat was a banquet that lasted for five days, and we savored many wonderful dishes. But my assistant was not with us when we returned to our homes in the early hours of Easter Day.

PART IV

BEARING WITNESS
TO
THE SYSTEM

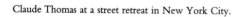
Claude Thomas at a street retreat in New York City.

— 24 —

I Vow Not to Kill

Peacemakers make vows and don't always keep them.

Vowing not to kill, we kill constantly. Vowing not to steal, we steal all the time. Vowing not to tell lies, we tell lies.

So what are these peacemaker vows, and why do we make them?

These vows represent profound personal commitments. Though they're similar to the Ten Commandments, they're not prohibitions or injunctions against doing something. Instead they embody the central aspects of our lives and form the deepest intentions of our hearts. We're stating a powerful intentionality to fulfill them by bearing witness to them in every situation that arises, day after day.

That's why they're preceded by the vows of unknowing, bearing witness, and healing. These first three vows lay out our path. They're guideposts telling us how to approach killing, stealing, lying, and anger. The very first guidepost is the vow to penetrate into unknowing. This means that we carry no preconceived notion about what killing is and what is right or wrong. We approach each killing situation anew, looking with a fresh eye at its ingredients.

Situations of killing arise every day, every

minute of our lives. In a retreat I led in 1996, one woman raised her hand and told me that since she's a vegetarian, and since she doesn't walk around shooting people, she has no issues connected with the vow not to kill. I told her to pay closer attention, because in the next five minutes she will surely kill.

Our survival depends on the deaths of other beings. Once again, I like to use my body as an example. My body is alive, yet at every moment things are born and destroyed inside. Whether I eat meat, vegetables, or fruit, enzymes are destroying these forms of life in order to convert them into nourishment. New cells are born and old cells die. When I get sick and take medication, I'm killing bacteria and viruses, which are living beings. If things don't die, I won't live.

The same thing happens in nature. Look at the live oak tree. Leaves die and new leaves get born. Branches wither and fall off while new shoots emerge. The tree itself is a microcosm of life and death, with tiny creatures living and dying in the grooves of its bark and inside the crevices of its trunk, consuming and being consumed. The oak tree lives, while parts of it are dying and getting born every moment.

With each step we take out in the country we destroy insects, and in the city our concrete destroys entire species of life. When we gather wheat to make bread we kill field mice. Our lives imply the deaths of others, just as others' lives imply our deaths. Bearing witness to killing and non-killing is bearing witness to the life and death of all sentient beings. We are one body, the Net of Indra. Seeing how many beings give their lives so that we may live, we get a renewed appreciation for our lives and a tremendous compassion for all life-forms on our planet. This leads to a minimizing of killing. If we see ourselves as the entire universe, with nothing excluded, we will naturally not wish to kill anything unnecessarily. That is the healing that arises out of bearing witness to the cycle of life and death.

— 25 —

I Vow Not to Blame Others:
Fleet Maull

Nothing lies outside the practice of bearing witness and making peace. This means that no matter what happens to us, we can always act as peacemakers. The possibility for healing exists everywhere, as long as we bear witness.

One example of this is our peacemaker priest Fleet Maull.

Fleet is currently serving a twenty-five-year prison sentence at the U.S. Medical Center for Federal Prisoners, a federal penitentiary near Springfield, Missouri. His indictment came down in May 1985 and he has been behind bars ever since. He was convicted in December 1985 for cocaine smuggling, conspiracy, and conducting an ongoing criminal enterprise—a drug "kingpin" charge. His earliest possible release date under the "kingpin" statutes is November 1999.

I met Fleet in the early 1990s and have tried to pay him a visit at least once a year. Since the penitentiary is far from where his family and friends live, Fleet gets only a couple of visits a year. From the first time he contacted me and wrote me about himself and his work, I knew Fleet Maull was a peacemaker. Like Claude Thomas, he had already established his path before I met him. In ordaining him, I gave a name to what was already there.

Originally from a Catholic, middle-class family, Fleet came of age in the 1960s. "By the time I graduated from high school in 1968," he says, "I was an angry, disillusioned young man with no faith in the religious, social, and political culture I'd been raised in. In college I literally majored in drugs, sex, and rock and roll, with a minor in antiwar politics."

In 1972 he began to explore Latin America, sailing along the coast of Central America and farming a small piece of land in the Peruvian Andes. By then he was involved in serious alcohol and drug abuse. Five years later, married and the father of a little boy, he returned to the United States and enrolled at the Naropa Institute, a Buddhist college in Boulder, Colorado. There he started a meditation practice, studied Buddhist and Western psychology, and met his Tibetan Buddhist teacher, the Venerable Chögyam Trungpa Rinpoche. Trungpa Rinpoche had an effect on Fleet that was similar to the effect the Vietnamese teacher Thich Nhat Hanh had had on Claude Thomas. Both teachers pointed the way to their students, each of whom had been living a life of addiction and alienation prior to meeting them.

Fleet's life of addiction to cocaine and alcohol continued, however. His marriage broke up. Periodically he'd make drug-smuggling trips to Latin America. He convinced himself that he had to do this in order to provide for himself and for his young son. "During those five years I lived two completely separate lives—a very public life as an apparently serious student of Buddhism attending intensive meditation programs all over North America, and a very secret life as a part-time drug smuggler and alcohol and cocaine abuser," he says.

He knew that he was under investigation well over a year before the indictment finally came down in 1985. He even seriously considered disappearing, leaving the country. When he finally broke down and spoke to his teacher and other trusted friends about his predicament, the consensus was that he should stay and face his legal problems squarely. This was a situation he would have to deal with sooner or later, and running away was not the answer. "I settled in for what I would have to face—for the rather scary bed I had made for myself," he says. He also finally entered a substance abuse treatment program.

As soon as he was indicted he gave himself up to the authorities. Denied bail, he spent seven months in a county jail awaiting trial and sentencing.

"It was a really hellish environment—a small, completely sealed tank, all welded steel inside a concrete flat-roof building. There were no windows, no ventilation, no place to walk around. It was overcrowded and incredibly hot. There was constant noise and chaos, yelling, arguing, four or five televisions going twenty-four hours a day—a totally crazy environment. That's where I started sitting on a daily basis for the first time."

Fleet's trial lasted three weeks. It was not what he'd expected. He'd pleaded guilty to smuggling drugs and knew he'd end up going to prison, but he denied the "kingpin" charge. Several close associates cooperated with the government lawyers in order to avoid prison or get reduced sentences, and testified against him. When the jury came back it found him guilty on all counts, and Fleet was sentenced to twenty-five years in prison, fifteen years before consideration of release. That was in December 1985.

One of the hardest peacemaker vows is the vow not to blame others. It is very human to deny responsibility for our lives. And since our lives involve other people from the minute we are born, it is very human to lay the responsibility for our lives on their doorsteps.

"It would have been very easy for me to become lost or stuck in anger and blaming," Fleet says, remembering the time after his conviction. "But the basic issue is accepting responsibility for the situation you're in—not guilt, but responsibility. Then you don't get involved in a lot of blaming—feeling persecuted, oppressed, and abused, and seeing the institution, authority, and the world as your absolute enemies. The most effective strategy for me was to take complete responsibility for everything that had happened and for everything that I would continue to experience, even in situations with a clear and significant involvement of others."

This was a time of intense suffering for Fleet. Imprisoned inside a crowded county jail, far from friends and supporters, confronted by former friends testifying against him under promise of immunity, he was tempted to give in to anger and blaming. But in taking responsibility for his life and for the consequences of his actions, in not blaming others, Fleet was coming from a place of unknowing. If he'd *known* that the trial was unfair, the sentence unjust, the people and society unscrupulous, if he'd *known* how terrible a twenty-five-year sentence in prison could be, there would have been no bearing witness, only the sense of being crushed by events beyond his control. Fleet chose unknowing. He was open to everything and experienced a heightened awareness and spaciousness even when the verdict was announced.

He says, "I was possessed by this time with a profound remorse for all the terrible pain, harm, and chaos I'd caused and all the pain my incarceration would continue to inflict on my family, especially my son, a nine-year-old boy, now without a father. I also had an intense desire to transform myself, to actively cultivate the profound teachings and blessings I had received from my teachers, as well as the values my parents had given me. And I felt compelled to do something beneficial with my energies and talents. The clearer my awareness became through living free from drug and alcohol abuse and through ongoing meditation practice, the more shocked I became at how drastically I had wasted energy, time, and talent; how I had wasted my life. I was driven to make up for lost time."

— 26 —

Peacemaker Vows in Prison

As soon as Fleet arrived at the federal penitentiary in Springfield, Missouri, he became a bilingual tutor teaching GED and ESL classes to other inmates. He tutored inmates who couldn't read and became a certified literacy trainer.

At first he was placed in a cramped, overcrowded dormitory with twenty-five other people. "I tried to describe what prison was like to a visiting friend," he remembers. "I told her to imagine cramming as many bunk beds as possible into her living room and two bedrooms and then rounding up the loudest, most inconsiderate people she could find to move in with her on a permanent basis."

This was especially hard for him because he wanted a place in which to meditate. Finally he cleaned out one of the sanitation closets, taking out mops, brooms, and trash barrels every day, setting them outside, taking a chair into the closet, and sitting there for an hour or two. During the summer the closet was like a sauna. He would sit with sweat pouring down his face and into his eyes. After two and a half years he finally got a single cell.

Two months after his arrival he began a Buddhist meditation group with the help of two other

Buddhist prisoners and has continued to coordinate the group for years, teaching meditation to hundreds of prisoners. When he began to receive letters from Buddhist prisoners throughout the country asking for encouragement and help, he realized the need for a support network for such prisoners. So Fleet founded Prison Dharma Network, a not-for-profit organization providing Buddhist literature, contacts, and resources to Buddhist prisoners everywhere, in 1989.

The Springfield penitentiary is a major federal prison hospital. About seven hundred of the eleven hundred inmates are medical patients. "When I arrived here in December 1985," Fleet says, "I was immediately struck by the amount of suffering. Out in the yard and in the halls you'd see people in wheelchairs. You'd see people using canes, walkers, and crutches, people who were obviously emaciated from cancer and other illnesses. Even though I was overwhelmed by being sentenced to twenty-five years in prison, I was still struck by that sight. It was helpful for me to realize that a lot of people had it much worse than I did."

In those years, as the AIDS epidemic was coming to light, inmates with HIV or AIDS were routinely isolated from the rest of the prisoners. This was done to protect the patients rather than the other prisoners, for there was fear of reprisals against AIDS patients due to ignorance about the disease. Fleet joined forces with a paraplegic patient who had already begun to talk to the prison administration about an inmate-staffed hospice program. Soon outside hospice professionals came in to conduct classes. With their staff sponsors, they developed a six-month pilot program, the first such inmate-staffed hospice program in American prisons.

Eventually the prison authorized a group of ten inmates, including Fleet, to work with dying inmates in Springfield.

"We began training in 1987, and in January of 1988 we started seeing patients," Fleet says. "We became surrogate family members, just being there so the patient knew that someone cared. We couldn't change the prison hospital, we couldn't change the typical attitudes that exist in a prison. But we could be a friend. That's really what the hospice was to begin with: just being there for the person. It's evolved into more than that now, with more nursing and medical staff involvement."

More professional training was given. Fleet became a trained hospice worker, then an instructor for other inmate hospice volunteers. Half of their clients were dying from AIDS, the other half from cancer.

When he began to work with dying inmates, Fleet came across his old friend, anger, once again. Since his incarceration in 1985 he'd worked hard on the vow not to be angry. Now he was working with other people who were angry, people who were dying.

"Dying in prison is, in some sense, the ultimate mark of failure in your life. Dying inmates want out. Their greatest hope is to survive their illness until they finish their sentence, or to receive a compassionate early release. They want to be cured or let out to die. They don't want to die in prison."

Over and over, Fleet worked with inmates who were angry about dying and not getting an early release date. One man, whom he calls John, a fifty-five-year-old inmate with lung cancer, actually had an early medical release overturned by the parole board because the prison doctors reported that he was responding to chemotherapy. He was obsessed with fighting that decision in the courts. After a while he withdrew, eating so little that the doctors, insisting that the chemotherapy was working and that the cancer was in remission, believed he was purposely trying to deteriorate so that he could get an early release. Eventually his health did deteriorate to such an extent that he got released. Three days later he died in a hospital close to his home.

The bitter irony for dying prison inmates is that they're caught in a double bind. "Their only chance of early release is deterioration to the point that death seems imminent," Fleet explains. "Any sign of improvement diminishes that chance. Patients often exhaust themselves in these efforts, becoming angry and bitterly resigned to dying in prison."

Fleet cared for many patients, like John, who were consumed by rage and bitterness at the prospect of dying behind bars. Some dealt with their anger in other ways, opening up and accepting his support. Some looked for religious solace, requesting and receiving prayer and pastoral service (Fleet found himself reciting Catholic prayers, something he hadn't done since he was a child, with dying inmates). And some chose to die alone.

Fleet bore witness to anger by founding a new ministry. In 1991, he founded the National Prison Hospice Association (NPHA) to help develop prison hospice programs staffed by inmates all over the country. Since that time, the NPHA has helped develop over a dozen prison hospice programs using inmate volunteers in state prisons all across the country. In addition, the association makes presentations at national conferences, develops training curriculums, and provides in-service training programs at different correctional institutions.

Getting prison authorities to agree to let inmates serve as hospice volunteers, rather than using outside volunteers, was a critical issue. One of the chaplains at Springfield, a prison chaplain for over twenty years, called the transformation of inmate hospice volunteers the biggest rehabilitation he'd ever seen.

"In prison there's a tremendous pull toward despair, hopelessness, and depression," Fleet says. "There's not a lot of pleasure, enjoyment, and happiness here because you're completely cut off from family, loved ones, friends, and nature, and there's no loving and nurturing going on. There's plenty to make you cave in and surrender to despair at any moment, especially if you're doing a long sentence like I am."

Fleet has witnessed terrible suicides by inmates who felt there was nothing more to live for. But his spiritual practice has sparked a high level of confidence. So has his service to dying inmates. "Hospice work has helped me discover human dignity," Fleet says. "This may not be the only way of discovering our dignity, but it's the one that worked for me." And he adds, "I feel completely inspired by my path here."

As of the writing of this book, Fleet Maull is still at the Springfield federal penitentiary. He continues to work as a full-time bilingual GED tutor and as a hospice volunteer. He is also completing a Ph.D. program in psychology. He is one of the busiest people I know, but he is no different from you and me; the rigors and trials of prison life are as tough for him as they are for everybody else. It's how he deals with them that's different. He sees everything that comes up—each event, each feeling—as an opportunity for new practice.

For instance, working with the vow not to steal can be very complex in prison. There are questions such as whether or not to participate in a black market that can furnish you with everything from hot, restaurant-quality meals, complete with linen napkins and cutlery, to new prison clothes. Fleet avoids this hustling side of prison life as much as he can, but he adds, "Like it or not, this convict world is my community. Something as simple as a birthday party for a friend is bound to involve some black-market food." He tries to balance the vow not to steal with his general vows to serve others.

Although he stopped using drugs and alcohol before his incarceration and continues to attend recovery meetings in the prison, intoxicants continue to be an issue for Fleet. An intoxicant can be anything that takes us away from our experience of day-to-day life, including one of the biggest experiences of all in prison life: boredom. Inmates love to do anything that will provide relief from boredom—compulsive eating, incessant TV watching, smoking, gambling, fighting. All of these can be intoxicants, taking us away from our present moment. Fleet avoids compulsive eating and late-night snacking in an effort to simplify, which in turn brings a quality of spaciousness into his life.

It's not easy. "There are still times when I wonder why I am doing this," he confesses. "Sometimes when I see and smell the prisoners preparing the standard late-night snack of nacho chips and cheese sauce heated in the microwave, I long for this momentary relief from boredom and loneliness. Sometimes I would just like to forget the whole thing and spend my time hanging out, watching TV, reading novels."

Fleet Maull's life is one of unlimited compassion. His work as a peacemaker behind bars arises out of his fearless bearing witness to the causes and effects of his own life. Prison life is as terrible for him as it is for others. He's been in the "hole"; he's faced dangerous physical confrontations. He's watched dying inmates fighting the system and fighting death till the last moment, passing out of this existence in rage and bitterness.

"How do we argue compassion for ourselves?" Fleet says, trying to explain why all of us should care about the life of prison inmates. "The makings for every despicable thing are in all of us. Our ability to accept ourselves hinges on our having healing relationships with those we want to shut out of our lives."

— 27 —

Bearing Witness
to the System

As I said earlier, when I first visited the Letten drug park in Zurich, I was struck by how close it was to the center of town. This place of deep suffering, anger, and greed lay only a short walk away from one of the world's great capitals of commerce, its painful profits within easy reach of the banks, businesses, and shoppers on the streets. It was like a diseased nerve, full of pain, attached to numerous veins and capillaries that transported the disease, in different forms, to all parts of Zurich, and even the world. These veins and capillaries were related to each other and to the sick nerve, just as they would be in our own bodies. In treating the disease, however, the Zurich government had sent in drug counselors for the drug users, neglecting to treat the other less obvious symptoms and locations of the disease.

If you don't think this strange, consider how we take care of our bodies. If I have heart disease, I don't cut my heart out of my body because it's not functioning the way it should. First a surgeon may insert a pacemaker to support the ailing organ, or alternatively provide new valves or perform a bypass operation. I'll improve my diet and exercise. I'll work less and rest more. I'll study stress reduction. My entire lifestyle will change in order to take care of the disease. Or if I develop melanomas, the doctors will probably treat the skin tumors with radiation. In addition, they may also apply chemotherapy and drug therapy in case the cancer has spread to other parts of my body. In any case, we treat the entire body, not just the most visible manifestation of the disease, and this treatment results in the transformation of the entire system.

We don't do this in healing our society. Drug users may be our social melanoma, but instead of treating the entire community we treat addicts like outlaws and hack away at them with laws and prohibitions, as if by shaking them off we will have treated the disease. And then we look away, as if they are no longer connected to us. We'd think it was suicidal for a person to act that way with a physical disease, but this is exactly what we do with poverty, disease, hunger, and discrimination. Because we don't see ourselves as one body. These diseases affect our entire system. So in order to heal them, we must bear witness to their presence in every part of our one body.

I call this bearing witness to the society in which we live, or bearing witness to the system.

I remember once driving home from New York City with a Sufi imam, a tall, thin African-American. As we approached southwest Yonkers late at night we saw lots of school-age boys on the streets. They were hanging out on the street corners talking, smoking, oblivious to the lateness of the hour when they should have been home. When I turned I found my companion's eyes full of tears.

"You see these boys?" he said. "By the time they're twenty most of them will be dead, in jail, or on drugs. I was there; I know."

My friend was bearing witness not just to his own life and the lives of the young men on the streets, but to an entire system which marginalizes African-American men.

A short time after that another associate of the Peacemaker Order, an African activist from Cameroon who works with homeless people in New York City, told me that as a boy, he, too, had spent a lot of time outside his home. He had been brought up in a Cameroon village culture, shaped by entirely different values and traditions. When he had come of age, he and boys like him were taken out of the village and taught to be homeless for many months, as a rite of passage. In both cases the boys were away from home and family, without parental supervision. But the circumstances were very different, producing very different results. You can't bear witness to the differences in these lives without bearing witness to the vast differences in the systems.

If we truly bear witness to the wholeness of life, then we will bear witness not just to our own lives but to the complex functioning of society as a whole.

When we began the Greyston Family Inn with a plan to build transitional housing for homeless families, the first site we considered was an abandoned school, comprising two buildings, right in the middle of our neighborhood. The city of Yonkers called it School 6. The buildings had stood empty and unused for nine months, and the mayor, Angelo Martinelli, wished to give them to us. Our neighbors, however, opposed the project, saying they didn't want more homeless families to come into the neighborhood. So I began to make the rounds of local churches, introducing myself to the various ministers. I brought with me our architectural plans for the site and described our proposed programs, hoping to persuade them that the families coming in would not be a drain on our community.

Some were noncommittal. Others were hostile. Finally, I met one Baptist minister who liked our ideas and plans. He and I developed a warm personal rapport, but he warned me that it would take no less than thirty years for his parishioners to accept me. "You don't look like us, you don't eat our food, and you don't talk like us," he said to me.

He was pointing out that it wasn't enough to have great ideas and the resources to carry them out. We were part of a system. We lived in a city with strong racial tensions and mistrust. It wasn't enough for me to visit everyone and try to see things from their points of view—or to try to help them see things from my point of view. We also had to bear witness to a system of racism, poverty, and disempowerment. We were all part of it, we had formed it together, and it, in turn, was now forming our views and reactions. So no matter what good work we did, it would take thirty years to gain the trust of the community, simply because I was white rather than African-American, a Buddhist rather than a Baptist.

If we were to see someone being stabbed on the

street, most of us would probably run to get the police and point out who did it. But if you're a prison inmate and you see someone getting stabbed you won't identify the stabber because that's snitching, punishable by death according to inmates' rules. So if you see a stabbing, you can't take care of it without bearing witness to the system.

Most of the time we don't do that. Some bear witness to a few ingredients; most of us look away. It's the rare individual who's ready to see all the ingredients and how they interconnect. Just think of the Letten. One peacemaker can visit the Letten and will see only the suffering of the drug users. So she will begin a drug rehab program. Another will see the suffering of the dealers, too, so he will try to persuade them to put away their guns and get another job. If he's a minister he may talk about the evil of their ways and the need for repentance. But say a peacemaker comes into the Letten and bears witness to the entire system, from the users to the dealers to the banks to the businesses to the citizens to the government that carefully supervises such a system. She will see how money from drugs permeates the economic and social life of the city and the world. What will she do then? She will try to change the entire system.

The peacemakers we remember and honor most are those who try to heal our society as a whole, not just pieces of it. Instead of donating money to a food pantry, they try to eliminate hunger. Instead of serving the homeless a Thanksgiving Day meal, they try to eliminate homelessness and poverty. They can't help it. Once they bear witness to the functioning of an entire society, the healing that arises is on the scale of an entire society. During this process they challenge every human being and institution, as well as our very way of life. And they're often killed for it.

The old Jewish prophets bore witness day by day to the transgressions of Israel, and some were put to death. Christ was crucified because He witnessed and tried to heal the corruption and denial of the general society. Mahatma Gandhi's insistence on nonviolence affected not just the Indians and the British but Nelson Mandela and his supporters in South Africa, Martin Luther King Jr. and his supporters in America, and peacemakers everywhere. Gandhi also directly affected people around the world who believed in violence, who had old scores to settle, who made money out of weapons, or who felt that certain wars were justified. Is it any wonder that he was assassinated?

Closer to home, when Father Bruce Ritter started Covenant House in New York City's Times Square as a shelter for runaway youth, local drug dealers put out a contract on his life. In taking care of young runaways, he had removed them as potential users, pushers, and hustlers from city streets, thus threatening the dealers' profits. The parts of the system around Times Square were so interconnected that although Father Ritter only worked with one piece, he was simultaneously affecting all of the other pieces, too. For years he was protected by bodyguards wherever he went.

Bearing witness is a dangerous business. Once we start it's hard to stop. A peacemaker's life often starts with a single encounter, a single witnessing. Soon there's a second and a third. After a while we can't look away. We see not only hunger, illness, and racism, but the people, institutions, and societies that benefit from them. The healing that arises threatens the very foundation of these societies. We will be called troublemakers, we'll be called Communists. And sometimes we'll be arrested, beaten, or killed.

28

Bearing Witness to
Our Systems of Survival

After Russian troops liberated Auschwitz in January 1945, many of the survivors committed suicide. This happened among survivors of other camps as well. There were many reasons why people who'd lived through the horrors of the camps killed themselves after liberation, usually to do with overwhelming feelings of loss, grief, and guilt.

But I believe that some killed themselves for another reason, too. In order to survive the Auschwitz system, they had developed a system of survival. With the help of this system they'd lived through starvation, disease, exposure, and systematic selections and extermination. But this system was designed to help them survive Auschwitz, not life after Auschwitz. When Auschwitz ended and a new life began, they felt unprotected, at a loss, unable to deal with the new system. So they put an end to their life.

In some way we're no different from those survivors. Each of us has a system of survival. It comes out of our conditioning, from patterns we developed early in life. In fact, one way of looking at our society is that it's a conglomerate of all our individual survival systems. Each such personal system becomes our custom-made suit of armor, designed to protect us as we make our way through society, the bigger system. Each new social situation is a new system, and for each new system we try to create a new suit of armor. But like those Auschwitz survivors who killed themselves at the end of the war, we don't always succeed.

Shortly after our 1996 Auschwitz retreat, I read the story of Binjamin Wilkomirski, who spent his early childhood at a concentration camp in Poland. His memoir, *Fragments,* was one of the most moving accounts of survival in the camps that I'd ever encountered. In the system in which he spent his childhood years, the Majdanek concentration camp, there was no such thing as mother. There were no such things as Nazis or guards, just "black boots," and there were certainly no such things as warm clothes or a full stomach. Beatings, starvation, and death were the everyday experiences.

Most revealing of all was his account of growing up in Switzerland after the war, first in an orphanage and then with an adoptive family that had no idea about where he came from. He writes of staring at fresh slices of bread, not touching them though he was very hungry. According to his old system of survival, a pile of fresh slices of bread was nothing other than a trap set by the "black boots" so that they could kill him. For months he wouldn't lie on his bed, only under it. A bed, too, was a trap. When the orphanage group assembled outside to walk in the snow and he couldn't find his boots, he hurriedly wrapped newspapers around his bare feet and rushed out to join them, convinced that if he didn't he'd be killed. The other orphans and teachers, brought up in a different system, laughed.

His old system of survival reappeared even a few years later, when he went skiing for the first time with his classmates. As a little child he'd seen the small bodies of his friends loaded onto coal cars in Majdanek and taken from a small hut up a narrow rail track to the peak of a cone-shaped mountain. There the cars disappeared into an opening on top of the mountain, and when they came back they were empty. The bodies went in and never came out. Now, in Switzerland, he watched as his classmates were hooked onto a rope at a hut in the valley and then swooped up the mountain slope two by two. When they reached the top of the mountain they glided inside a huge, open black hole and disappeared. When the double hooks came back downhill, they were empty.

The young Wilkomirski did everything he could to avoid being hooked to the rope and taken up the mountain. His survival system told him that this was a death machine and that the man trying to hook him to the rope was his executioner. He fell down on the snow each time the hook came up behind him. The man cursed him, and still the boy wouldn't stand straight and get hooked to the rope. Finally the ski instructor gave up, told him to get off the platform, and then yelled after him, "City kid...weakling...scaredy-cat!"

Our interaction with society is a constant feedback mechanism. We are always exchanging feedback with society and then adjusting our private survival system accordingly, to the degree that we can.

During a time of war, soldiers are encouraged to kill as many people as possible. When these same soldiers return home they find that, much like Auschwitz survivors, they're living in a new system where there's no room for the instincts they developed during wartime. Some can't adjust their personal systems. The result is that society considers them misfits and rejects them, and many end up in VA institutions or on the streets. Claude has told me that more American soldiers committed suicide since the war than were killed during the war.

Elie Wiesel related in his book on the death camps that when he and his father were running in the snow after being evacuated by the SS from Auschwitz, he wished his father would fall and die so that he, younger and unencumbered by the older man, might live. His book bears witness not just to the Auschwitz system, but also to his own system of survival and its implications for the relationship between father and son.

When I worked at McDonnell-Douglas as an aerospace engineer, there were major layoffs one year due to cutbacks in government defense spending. Many of my colleagues who were laid off went through massive depression. They couldn't cope with even small things, like taking care of their own lawns instead of relying on a gardener. But just a few years back, before they'd begun to make large salaries, they had done their own gardening. They had managed with small incomes and starter houses. Now they couldn't adjust.

One of our peacemaker vows is not to lie. Lying has a lot to do with the systems we inhabit. Most of us don't knowingly lie; we simply tell the truth as we see it, dictated by our system of survival. But in other people's eyes, according to their system, the truth we tell is a lie.

I remember one particular meeting during the time I visited Yonkers churches, trying to acquaint people with our proposed community projects. One evening a man heckled me from the beginning, not letting me talk, accusing me of making millions of dollars off the backs of poor people. I denied it, he said it again, and we both got angrier and angrier. Finally he yelled that I was a pimp and that my plan was to bring homeless mothers out of the motels (then used to house homeless families) and into our bakery, where they would work as slaves, and when we were finished with them we were going to put them back into the motels. I lost my temper and yelled back: "Bullshit!"

Later on I remembered the words of my minister friend. I didn't look like the man who'd heckled me; I didn't talk or dress like him. For years he'd fought a system where people who looked like me kept him at the margins of society. He'd developed a personal survival system for self-protection, and according to that system I was a pimp. According to mine, I was not and he was lying.

We lie whenever we think we're telling the truth. For there is no truth. There's only the truth as we see it. I'm color-blind. I see something purple, you may see it green. Am I wrong? That's how I see it. Are you wrong? That's how you see it. Change the person and the truth is different. Change the system and the truth is different once again. All we can do at any given moment is respond to the person at that moment; the response will change depending on the person, the situation, the moment, and the system.

This is particularly important in connection with people in authority. When I express myself, people think I'm laying out the truth. What I'm writing in this book is not the truth, it's simply the way I see certain things. You're not wrong if you see them differently. When you and I meet and we listen to each other—not out of knowing that the other person lies but out of unknowing—we're working with the vow not to lie.

When we live out of unknowing we're shedding our suit of armor. Each time we let go of our fixed ideas about ourselves and others, we're letting go of our individual system of survival. For these systems may have once helped us survive, but now they are destroying us. They are destroying our ability to act spontaneously, to respond directly, to take care of any situation that arises.

Living out of unknowing, we are naked. We go from one situation to the next, from one person to another, from one system to another, and we respond to each directly and appropriately. One day we have a job, the next we don't. One day we have our family around us, the next we've lost someone we love. When we live from unknowing we have no expectations of what will be and how we will feel. We are disarmed, going from one situation to the next, and bearing witness.

PART V

THE MAKING
OF
A PEACEMAKER ORDER

Joan Halifax on the day of her ordination, 1997.

29

Joan Halifax, or the Making of a Peacemaker Robe

Our Peacemaker Order includes both lay people and priests. All are peacemakers and take peacemaker vows. All sew peacemaker robes.

Shakyamuni Buddha, after his great enlightenment experience, went on to teach for almost fifty years. He wandered from one town to another in India, accompanied by his disciples, a group of mendicant monks. Each of these monks had to leave home. They owned nothing and relied on the generosity of strangers. When they were on the road, which was for most of the year except during the rainy season, they wore only their robes and carried only their begging bowls and enough coins to pay for cremation if they died.

In the beginning they dressed like other religious practitioners of the time. The story goes that one day a king requested of Shakyamuni Buddha that his monks wear robes that would identify them as the Buddha's disciples. The Buddha agreed. One day he stopped to look at a rice field. He noticed that it was crisscrossed by footpaths that were orderly and neat, and that the rice plants grew together peacefully with the other creatures in the field. The Buddha pointed to the rice field and asked Ananda, one of his senior disciples, to create a robe like the pattern of the rice field. Ananda created a robe made up of long and short pieces of discarded fabric that were then dyed and sewn together into panels, and this became the robe of the Buddha's monks.

The rule was that the monks could use only materials that had been rejected by the rest of society. These included fabrics chewed by cattle or mice, burned by fire, and from clothing or shrouds of the dead. These materials were usually just thrown into the streets, but often the monks would visit charnel grounds to find the shrouds of the dead. They would put aside the parts that were torn and wash and dye the rest. Then they stitched the pieces together into panels. The panels were then stitched together and enclosed inside a border. In this way they sewed their robe out of panels, each panel made of fragments of fabrics discarded by the rest of society.

In our Peacemaker Order peacemaker priests sew one robe prior to their ordination, a robe of seven panels. They can't buy material for this robe or use anything new. Instead, they have to obtain from their friends and families pieces of fabric from clothing and articles no longer in use, pieces that would be thrown away. These are then dyed and sewn together by hand into a peacemaker robe, a process that usually takes several months.

One novice priest did something a little different from the others. She visited the charnel grounds of our modern society—the AIDS hospices and cancer wards, the places of alcoholism and disease—and got the makings of her robe there, just like the Buddha's monks 2,500 years ago.

Joan Halifax is a peacemaker priest. Joan was already a prominent Buddhist teacher when we first talked about her joining the Zen Peacemaker Order. In fact, she'd already received the Lamp Transmission from Thich Nhat Hanh, empowering her to be a lay priest and teacher. In addition, Joan is a national figure in the training of social and hospice workers, as well as the general public, in contemplative care of the dying.

Joan is full of energy and enthusiasm. Her visits to Yonkers are usually brief stops during her long and arduous trips across the country to lead conferences, workshops, and retreats. She is a vigorous, beautiful woman who leads groups into the wilderness on retreat. But this hasn't always been the case.

"I have not been a physically healthy person," she says. "At the age of four I had a severe viral infection and was blind for two years. Then there were two very serious car accidents and various illnesses that laid me low."

She began to work actively with dying people in 1970. Her calling grew out of her relationship with her grandmother. An artist, painter, and sculptress, Joan's grandmother designed beautiful tombstones for a Savannah graveyard. She would often dress the hair of her deceased friends or pick out their clothing after they'd died. She loved to tell her granddaughter ghost stories. She also told her how she was taking care of her friends who were dying.

Joan's grandmother died in the 1960s. "At that time dying was a medical event. Doctors saw their training as a kind of warrior training against the enemy that was Death. They saw dying people as threats to their medical expertise. My grandmother was put in a nursing home. I remember visiting her with my father and her begging my father to help her die. I felt so helpless in the face of that suffering. When she did die I looked into the coffin and saw her face finally relaxed, and I promised her I would do everything I could to help people die well."

She began to provide contemplative care for dying people. She did this for many years, sometimes with people she knew well, other times with people who had heard of her work and wanted her help in the dying process. In the mid-1980s she began to work with men dying from AIDS. "That was a very good experience for me because I was working with men who wanted to die well, who wanted to be an example for other men who were homosexual and who had AIDS. Conscious dying was important to them. They taught me a lot."

By the time she became a peacemaker priest, Joan Halifax had been working with the dying for more than twenty-five years. Currently operating out of the Upaya Center in Santa Fe, New Mexico, she designs and delivers training programs to hospice workers, social workers, and others on the contemplative care of dying people.

Since Joan is constantly on the road, she was shocked to hear that she would have to sew a peacemaker robe by hand prior to her ordination. It would be a lot of work, and she was unaccustomed to sewing. But she decided to do it.

She also made a decision on where to get the pieces that would make up her robe. "I thought that for me, the best thing would be to go to people whom I really cared for, people who were ill, people who were dying, relatives and friends of those who'd died, elders, and ask them for a pillowcase, an old dress, a handkerchief, any old rag that I could incorporate into my robe."

Making her peacemaker robe was not easy. For one thing, she had to ask for the pieces. "I had to beg. That was really hard to do because my usual way of being with people in grief is to serve them, not to ask them to give me something. This time I was the one doing the asking. I was begging of people who were wounded, people in mourning. I discovered that a certain kind of intimacy arises when you ask a favor of someone who's suffering. I felt embarrassed, I felt vulnerable. I was asked by a number of people who had given me fabric to listen to their stories. Others contacted me and said, 'I would like you to include my mother in your robe' or 'I would like you to include my partner in your robe.' One healthy old man who had been very kind to me over the years said, 'I want to be in your robe.' I said, 'But you don't have a catastrophic illness.' He said, 'But I have old age.'"

As she received the pieces she dyed them in a special dark dye consisting of black, dark green, and greenish rust, that interacted with the fibers rather than completely coating them. As a result, the fabrics acquired a blended, duller color. They weren't one single color—each piece came out a different shade with its own print and texture.

Then she did a rough cut. "I didn't want to cut up the beautiful dresses, the coats, the silk jackets. Some were things I would have loved to wear. Instead I had to take scissors to them. I had to cut up tablecloths, nightgowns, even an old wedding dress. We're engaged all the time in various forms of dismemberment—separating or taking things apart and then bringing things back together again into new ways of being."

And she made mistakes. "I cut some too small," she remembers. "But this is the practice of the situation. The mistakes, too, are part of the robe."

Then she began to stitch the dyed pieces together, creating seven panels. Each panel consisted of one short piece and two long pieces. She sewed a close friend's mother into her robe by using a large fragment of a magnificent green silk dress. She sewed her own mother into her robe by putting in a piece from the pillowcase on which her mother had rested her head for many years. She sewed in a bright red skirt sewn, but never completed, by a woman with multiple sclerosis. She sewed in a pajama top from a woman who'd died of breast cancer. She sewed in a piece of Balinese material worn by a man in Southeast Asia with testicular cancer. She sewed in a handkerchief belonging to a woman suffering from dementia.

"There are living people in my robe, there are dead people in my robe, there are people who have committed suicide in my robe. There are friends and family members in my robe. There are people who have died of cancer, of AIDS, and of heart disease in my robe. It has been a process of gathering together many forms of suffering."

Down in Santa Fe, eight women in her community came in to help her sew. For some it was a wonderful project, for a few others, very upsetting. The robe has a palpable presence, a manifestation of compassion, suffering, impermanence, and commitment.

Joan Halifax was ordained as a peacemaker

priest in 1997. She had been bearing witness to people's old age, illness, and death for many years. From that July day on she began to wear their pain and suffering as a second skin.

"It's like the AIDS quilt," she said. "It doesn't stretch across the Washington Mall, it stretches across my back. In a way we're all wearing the AIDS quilt. We're all sick, we all have AIDS, we all have cancer. Many of our mothers are dead. Many of our brothers are dead. This robe won't distinguish me from anyone. It'll connect me with everyone."

Like Joan Halifax, all peacemaker priests in the Peacemaker Order sew a robe out of patches. For some, like Joan, it's obvious where the pieces will come from. When my wife, Jishu, recently sewed a new peacemaker robe for herself, the pieces she took came from Pamsula, the company she started that recycles discarded fabrics into gorgeous appliqué and patchwork clothing and accessories. She wanted to have a robe reflecting her love and commitment to the Greyston community, which she had served for fifteen years.

Some novice priests don't know where their pieces should come from. For them, sewing their robes is a process of self-discovery. As the pieces come together and the robes take shape, the threads of their lives become apparent, and so does their calling. Each piece is an ingredient. The meal that arises in the end is not just a peacemaker robe, it's a teaching about how to live a peacemaker life, and those who wear these robes absorb this teaching with their entire bodies.

One novice, who wished to work in the inner-city Bronx, ended up gathering pieces for his robe from discarded clothes from his hometown in Puerto Rico and from bedsheets that were thrown away in Mexico City. Not till these pieces came in and he had begun to sew them together did he realize that he wanted to work not only with Latino communities in the Bronx but with communities in Latin America as well.

Fleet Maull couldn't assemble the pieces for his robe easily because he is still in prison. So he sent various letters around the country, and people sent in their offerings. People who had known him for many years, who knew him as a prison inmate, a prison hospice worker, a family man, a father, a friend, a devoted student of Tibetan Buddhism, and a cocaine dealer all made contributions. Together these pieces made a dazzling peacemaker robe.

And while all the pieces are dipped in similar dark dyes, and although the peacemakers follow the same sewing instructions and make the same careful stitches, each robe comes out looking startlingly different from every other. Each panel is unique. When the Peacemaker Order gathers, we all wear our unique robes, our individual offerings to the universe.

We don't have to be perfect to be peacemakers. Neither Joan, Claude, nor Fleet is perfect. They are not saints. Remember the Net of Indra, with a jewel at each node? Each peacemaker is that jewel. Each of us has all of the ingredients of a peacemaker, and these ingredients are nothing other than our lives. Out of the joy and suffering of our lives emerge certain qualities that shine, others that are dim, and still others that are repellent. In describing some of the people I've known and worked with, I'm highlighting their shining qualities. These qualities differ for each of us because we're all different, each with a distinct personality and characteristics. And we have one thing in common. Each of us is a jewel in the Net of Indra, and we all have qualities that shine brightly.

This means we don't have to wait to be perfect before we take action. We simply have to cook our peacemaking meal out of the ingredients we already have. The more we bear witness and act, the clearer these ingredients become. Whether we become peacemaker priests or not, the threads, stitches, and pieces of our peacemaker robes become more and more visible.

The point of our peacemaking is not to do a perfect job. The point is to bear witness, to offer, to be the offering at each moment. Of itself, the fruit is born. Each of us is that fruit in this wonderful garden that some call the universe.

30

The Zen
Peacemaker Order

When we sew our robes, we start from scratch. In the beginning, when all we have in front of us is just a few rags, we can't imagine what this robe will eventually look like. Some of us complain that we're not sewing it correctly, that the panels will come out crooked and the robe all wrong. Mostly we put aside our mental chatter and just sew the robe together, one piece at a time, one panel at a time.

Starting from scratch means starting from unknowing. You get a piece from here and you get a piece from there and you put them together. We have no idea how the end product will look. We may have a vision of how we'd like it to look, but we don't really know. This is a very hard practice, and if we can start with unknowing, with no right and no wrong, then there's no problem. Nothing can come out wrong.

When Jishu and I started the Zen Peacemaker Order we put it together in the same way that peace-makers sew their robes. We started from scratch. One piece came in, then another, and we stitched them together. Then a third piece came in, and we attached that to the first two. Like novice priests, we are also curious about what the whole thing will look like in the end.

The Peacemaker Order will never be complete, but several panels have already come together out of the people we've sewn into the order. Just as Joan sewed various people into her robe, Jishu and I have sewed a highly diverse group of peacemakers—including those I've described in these pages—into our robe that we call the Peacemaker Order. The order that emerges will be nothing other than the energies of these people, their lives, and their work.

In looking back, the first piece of this new robe, the first ingredient, was the vow I made in early 1994 on the steps of the U.S. Capitol. This was the only piece for a long time. During the next couple of years other responsibilities took my time and energy. By the early summer of 1996 we were ready to continue. At that time both Jishu and I were being paid by the Greyston Network. We decided to get off Greyston's payroll, though it was practically our only source of funds, because it was important for both of us to start from scratch. With no certain source of funds, no expectation of a bimonthly check, we were now free to look everywhere for help. I'd learned about life's generosity from our time on the streets and was sure that as soon as we opened our hands and let go of what we had, we'd begin to receive. And, in fact, upon hearing what we were doing, a few old friends and supporters immediately pledged some money to keep us going for the first few months.

The next question was where we would work. We both had had offices at Greyston for many years, but this no longer made any sense. So Jishu and I converted our house into office space for the new Peacemaker Order. It is a one-family home across the street from a Pentecostal church. The house has a small basement and attic. With the help of very minor renovations we created desk and computer space for six people. By the time we moved the order's offices to another site more than a year later, a dozen people were working out of our house every day. They'd come from around the world. Each person who worked with us, including social workers, artists, writers, and Catholic and Zen priests, as well as businesspeople, was another piece of the fabric, another fragment to be sewn into a panel of the Peacemaker Order.

Another early ingredient was the order's mission to serve as a home for peacemakers around the world. I began to talk with the different peacemakers I knew, and almost immediately people wanted to join. Claude Thomas, in Massachusetts, wanted to be part of the order. So did Joan Halifax in New Mexico. So did Fleet Maull, in the Springfield penitentiary. So did Pat O'Hara, a Buddhist teacher who works with people with AIDS in New York City. So did Paco Lugovina, who'd spent years building low-cost housing in the South Bronx. A network of social service organizations in Italy wanted to join, as did a group of Polish activists in Warsaw. No matter who I talked to, many wished to be part of our new order in some way. It didn't matter to them that it had just been founded, it didn't matter to them that we were still sewing the pieces together. They all wished to link their energies, stories, and training capabilities in order to become more effective peacemakers.

Many of these activists already had their own organizations, sometimes very big ones. They raised the question of how they could involve their groups with the order. The answer quickly turned up. Each such organization, each such group, would become a Peacemaker Village led by a Village Leader, a member of the Zen Peacemaker Order.

Originally, Jishu and I hadn't conceived of Peacemaker Villages. But in putting together the robe that we called the order and in putting out a call for pieces, activists from all walks of life, from around the world, both individually and in groups, came forward. In talking with them to see how they fit together, we soon realized that these activists made up a panel of Peacemaker Villages, with each peacemaker, each organization, another piece in the panel.

Other peacemakers, hearing about this opportunity, also wanted to link up with us, but not as members of a Zen Peacemaker Order. They didn't have a Zen practice, or else they were already ordained or practicing in a different religious tradition that prevented them from joining our order. For example, Fr. Niklaus Brantschen and Sr. Pia Gyger, founders of the Interreligious Peacemaker Union, a Swiss-based organization developing a new vision for interfaith dialogue and a world ethic, expressed interest in linking up with the order in mutually beneficial ways. So did Jon Kabat-Zinn, who does mindfulness-based stress management training at the University of Massachusetts Medical Center. Ministers, lawyers, and academics wanted to join and find a way of incorporating peacemaking into their work. Soon we realized that they, too, were forming a panel. Only this wasn't a panel of a robe called the Zen Peacemaker Order. This panel, which we eventually called the Interfaith Assembly of Peacemaker Villages, belonged to a new robe called the

Peacemaker Community. The assembly became the hub of all Peacemaker Villages, linking peacemakers and their organizations throughout the world who subscribed to the Three Tenets of unknowing, bearing witness, and healing. The Peacemaker Community included not only the order and the assembly, but also a training facility called the Peacemaker Institute and a House of One People for interfaith events and celebrations.

In the next few chapters I will describe the making of a few other panels of the Zen Peacemaker Order. Please keep in mind that each one of them started out of unknowing. During my years of work and travel, many people have told me that they want to do something. They want to put an end to poverty, disease, and discrimination. They want to create a better world, but they don't know where to start. They think they need answers before they can get to work.

If you are one of these, I dedicate this chapter, and the next few chapters, to you. If you want to do something, start with the few pieces that are right in front of you. If you feel you have nothing in front of you, then beg for them. Something will come. It may look like nothing: an apartment that needs fixing up, secondhand toys for a day care center, a senior citizen who wants to volunteer her time, used clothes for recycling, an abandoned school yard. Just start putting one piece together with another. Take as much time as you need. Don't worry about the final result.

One day you'll look over your work and be dazzled by your multipanel peacemaker robe.

31

Return to School 6

After we opened the order's offices in our home another question came up. Meditation/prayer was a regular practice of the Zen Peacemaker Order. Where were we going to do it?

For many years members of the Zen Community of New York had gathered daily for meditation. Where we gathered in the past had reflected our activities at the time. When we had been a retreat center situated in a large mansion in the community of Riverdale, we sat in a wood-paneled meditation hall. After that we sat in the third floor of the Greyston Bakery, across the street from a paint factory and just next door to an all-night club. Later we meditated in the basement of one of our residence buildings, and after that within the walls of a cloistered nunnery before it was converted into an AIDS housing complex.

Where would we sit now? We had no meditation hall or retreat facilities. Our own house had become a small office complex, and the other house that the order owned was filled to capacity as a residence for staff.

I started to walk the neighborhood. In a way this wasn't so different from looking for a place to gather during our street retreats. I wanted a place where members and candidates could come together in the morning for meditation or prayer before going on our separate ways. Just like we do on the streets. And there it was, right at the corner of the cul-de-sac where Jishu and I live.

School 6. A decade earlier we'd failed to acquire the abandoned two-building site for conversion into housing for homeless families. We had built Greyston housing on another site, and for ten more years School 6 languished. By now it had become the local junkyard, a dumping ground for the neighbors' garbage and trash, for empty soda and beer bottles thrown by pedestrians on adjoining Ashburton Avenue. It was also a drug haven. Though the school was fenced in, dealers and users met regularly in its front yard, hidden from view by tall weeds and wild grass. The ground was littered with needles and syringes.

At various times our block association and local church ministers complained about School 6. Over the years other organizations tried to acquire it with various plans, but School 6 had become a political football. So people walked away from it. The community tried to pretend it wasn't there. The school was left to rot. Pipes broke and water flooded both buildings. Furniture and equipment rusted. There was lead in the paint and asbestos everywhere, but that didn't prevent homeless people from spending their nights there or the neighborhood children from climbing and playing inside. School 6 had become a symbol of inner-city decay, of the disintegration that happens when people don't work together.

It was perfect for our meditation.

At first we had no key, so we got in through a

large hole in the fence in back of the school like every-one else. After a while the city administrators gave us a key so we could enter through the main gate. There were only a handful of us those first early mornings. The large front yard was so littered, so full of weeds and dense underbrush, that all we could do was sit on the stoop under the red school arch, hidden from the view of the people passing by on the street.

After a half hour of meditation we'd grab work gloves and plastic bags, a hoe, a rake, or a shovel, and get to work. While some people went up and down Ashburton Avenue collecting the trash that had accu-mulated overnight, others started to clear the over-grown school yard. First we cleared away large piles of trash, then we began to uproot the tall weeds and underbrush. This was slow and arduous work, till we got a phone call from the city. They'd heard we were cleaning up School 6. The upcoming Labor Day Weekend had been designated a community clean-up day. Did we need a Dumpster? We sure did, I told them. More important, we needed a weeder to take down the weeds. No problem, they said. We'd get not only a weeder but also a contingent of United States Marines, on loan to the city for the weekend, to help remove the weeds from School 6.

So by the end of Labor Day Weekend 1996, the front yard of School 6, hidden by weeds, brush, and tall grass for over ten years, was finally revealed to pedestri-ans and neighbors, its asphalt surface clean and bare, the mica gleaming softly under the sun.

We continued picking up the layers upon layers of trash that had collected in the asphalt cracks and on the surrounding earth. We also took some of the gray stones from the crumbling front wall and moved them down to the asphalt parking area and laid them in a circle. Here we sat in meditation each morning, in our gray-stone open-air meditation hall.

By now we'd become a larger group. Candidates and members of the order, friends, neighbors, and people who'd heard what we were doing all came to join us. Some even brought their children to help out.

I decided to try to clear out one classroom inside the school. This was much trickier than clearing the outside. The mildew and rust had long ago destroyed the cabinets, desks, stands, and other equipment stored inside the school. A dark dust had settled on everything, making it hard to breathe. Wearing special gloves and masks, we began to pull out whatever we could, leaving the junked equipment by the Dumpster outside. Soon it became clear that we needed more help. Claude Thomas arrived for a week. For seven days he plowed through the classroom in School 6, sometimes working alone and sometimes with two others. It was unseasonably hot that week, but Claude didn't stop, returning to our house only for a quick drink and a shower before going back. At the end of the week one entire classroom in School 6 had been cleared.

We cleaned and sat at School 6 till the first winter storms, listening to the trucks shifting gears as they drove slowly down the steep street, the horns of the school buses, the rock and salsa music and conversation from open windows, the radios of passing cars, the barking neighborhood dogs. We did this in rain, in shine, and in the early winter cold. I sat with my back to Ashburton Avenue, but I was told by the others that pedestrians walking up and down the street—mostly mothers taking their children to school in the morning—often gaped at our group. We must have been a sight, sitting on gray stones in a circle in a school yard that had been hidden from view for many years. Inside, School 6 was still neglected, still unused. But the front schoolyard was now so visible that it was no longer a viable hangout for drug dealers and users. At least on the outside, School 6, a community eyesore, had become part of the neighborhood once again.

Just as the ancient monks had found material for their robes in charnel grounds and village garbage heaps, we, too, found a piece rejected by society. It was right there in front of us, not a minute's walk from the house. Once we started sitting there we also had to take care of it. So we started to clean. After the raking, the weeding, the clearing of the underbrush, and the rolling of the large gray stones into a circle, only then, step by step, the panel had emerged.

We'd sewn School 6 into the Peacemaker Order.

As I said earlier, it was a little like going on the streets, even a little like the retreat at Auschwitz. This was no quiet, peaceful meditation hall. Each day there was more weeding and cleaning. Each day as we sat we took in the morning symphony of sounds, smells, and sights of the neighborhood. Each day we also witnessed the results of disharmony and neglect. And out of this raw experience, a quiet healing arose for the community and for School 6.

Sometime that first winter the local neighborhood ministers discussed making School 6 a local community center. Then the idea faded. The buildings were in terrible disrepair, and everyone knew that it was cheaper to tear them down and build anew than to clean them up and renovate. So to this date School 6 remains unused and abandoned.

And we still sit there.

— 32 —

Asking for Money:
the Practice of *Malas*

When the order began its operations there were training programs, bearing witness retreats, and new projects. There was an office—and a staff. We needed money. How would we sew money into the Peacemaker Order?

We could have continued to depend on friends and supporters. We could have raised money like other religious organizations. Instead, I once again bore witness to my time and experiences of the streets, and had the idea that all candidates and members be required to raise money by assembling a *mala*.

As you'll remember, when people wish to join me on the streets their first requirement is to assemble *malas,* which are strings of beads worn as bracelets or necklaces. Candidates and members of the order have to assemble *malas* of 108 beads. That means they have to find 108 people who will support their work by making donations to the order. They have to ask their families, friends, partners, business associates, anyone they can think of. The rule is that they can't pay for the beads themselves, they must ask other people to buy them.

They have to beg. Of all the rules we have—the tithing of income, work in a Peacemaker Village, commitment to regular practice and training—the hardest practice for most members is asking for money.

When Shakyamuni Buddha wandered around India 2,500 years ago with his mendicant monks, they begged for their food every day. Whatever they got, they were grateful for—whether it was vegetables and rice, a bucket of water, or verbal abuse. Whatever they received, they ate that day. They never saved anything for the following day. There was no reserve. Each morning they took up their bowls and went begging for their food all over again.

The practice of not accumulating things, of starting all over, is very powerful. There's nothing wrong with having things, it's just that we tend to get attached to them and then spend our time and energy protecting them. Most of our peacemakers are house-holders. They have families they need to support and jobs with which to support them. Some sit with us at School 6 in the early mornings and then go to work. Others, who live far away, wait for training intensives. Unlike the Buddha's monks, they have homes and bank accounts and credit cards.

This makes the practice of gathering *malas* even more important. It brings up vulnerability, dependency, and rejection. Peacemakers with stable families and homes, established in their careers, have to go out and put themselves at risk. And though all we're doing is making an offering, leaving it to our friends and families to decide whether they wish to participate or not, we take their decisions personally. We're afraid of rejection.

Joan Halifax, a longtime peacemaker, had a difficult time begging for pieces of material for her robe.

Some time before that, when she was in her early forties, Joan had eye surgery followed by radiation. The doctors didn't fractionate the dosage of radiation adequately. As a result, her eyes were burned and she was in eye bandages for months.

"I was living in a very sparse situation at the time," she remembered. "There was no plumbing. Since I couldn't see I needed people to help me with everything."

Some time after that she got very ill with intestinal problems, was put on a long course of antibiotics, then became very sick from the medicine and couldn't get out of bed. "For three months I felt completely done in," she said. "But for me it was very good to once again be helpless and have to ask for help. It's the thing that I really want the people I work with, the sick and dying, to learn: Asking somebody for help can open profound virtue and generosity in others."

The practice of asking for money is our way, in the Peacemaker Order, of remembering what it's like to need and ask for someone's help.

When Fleet Maull went to prison he needed money for his son. Working as a senior GED tutor paid him no more than $60 a month. He could have hustled like other inmates, finding illegal ways to make money. Instead he asked his family to help out. That was a big change for him. "It meant breaking a deeply ingrained pattern of refusing to ask anyone for help and looking for a way to make a quick buck instead. It's been a positive change for me, and I know it's been better for my son, too."

Asking people for money is one way of working with the vow not to be stingy. When we don't ask, we don't let others give. When we fear rejection, we don't let generosity arise. As that old rabbi said to the man sitting at my table during the Brooklyn wedding many years ago, we're not letting others do a *mitzvah,* a good deed.

There's also the public aspect of *mala* practice. One of our peacemaker priests who works in the Bronx once said, "Raising the hundred and eight beads is the least part of it. The important thing is the journey I take to raise it and the journey the other person takes, the one who's listening to me."

Gathering a *mala* is taking a journey. We go out and talk to everyone we meet about our work. We don't hide in the closet or keep it private, we take a public stand about what we're doing. And that's hard for some people. We've had candidates who wished to keep their participation in the order separate from their professional work, their families, and their friends. They wanted to keep it private.

But what's private? What's public? All private things become public. When two people are deep inside a cave gossiping about someone, that gossip is heard around the world. I once served in an organization where the top officers met to decide something important. When we ended the meeting someone said, "Now don't say anything outside because people will get upset." "Don't worry, they already know," I told him.

We spend a great deal of energy keeping things private. In doing that we keep our efforts small and constricted. If we don't share our peacemaking with the universe, we won't receive the gifts the universe has to offer, gifts to make our work easier and more effective.

When we talk about the order, about sitting in School 6, street retreats, and Peacemaker Villages, we're making a tremendous offering to our families and friends. We're sharing a banquet with them, with rich and exotic dishes they never knew existed. In many cases they want to know more. Sometimes they buy beads. Sometimes they sit with us at School 6 and help us clean it up. Or else they join us on the streets, or get involved with the work of Joan Halifax or Claude Thomas. If we deny them these possibilities, we are being stingy.

Some people tell me that it's not in their temperament to ask. I tell them that to be effective peacemakers they have to ask. I'm probably a loner by temperament. As a little boy, I disliked parties and big groups. Given the choice, I always preferred to be on my own or with one or two friends. Once I became a peacemaker my entire life became networking with lots of people, often working with very large groups. In fact, some people have said that I am a magnet that attracts the energy of many activists and teachers. That didn't happen by temperament. It happened because sharing my goals and dreams with the entire universe is the only way I know of making them come true.

Finally, I would like to say one more thing about the importance of asking, this time asking things of yourself. Over and over again I run into people who tell me they want to make peace but that they have to learn more, know more, become better people, or become enlightened before they can start working on behalf of others. For me, that's the state of being stingy. Each of us is more than qualified to do peacemaking. Each of us, as we are, is full of beautiful gifts. Every person who's reading these words has wonderful resources right now. So why shouldn't we share them?

If you're hungry you go into the kitchen and look in the refrigerator to see what you can pull together for a meal. If you look and say, "There isn't enough of this" or "I don't have that, and therefore I won't eat," that's the condition of being stingy. And if we keep doing that we'll die.

If you want to do something but don't feel empowered, learn to ask—of yourself and of other people. Don't be stingy with who you are!

— 33 —

The Day of Reflection

One day a month we take a break from our peacemaking work and bear witness to our own lives. We use our vows to look at ourselves and share what we see with other members of the order. We also fast after the noon meal. We call it our Day of Reflection.

We recite our vows at the beginning of the day and spend the rest of it examining how we have practiced them. Why? Because it's easy not to. It's easy to keep busy in so many ways that we don't look at ourselves. The purpose of this day is to bear witness to our issues, which are none other than the ingredients of our lives. Our ability to heal the world—our Supreme Meal—is made up of these ingredients.

We try to do these reflections as a group, sharing who and what we are. There's no religious authority present.

Since the days of Shakyamuni Buddha, monks have taken vows to uphold a monastic way of life. But it was also common for lay people, who did not take such vows and who lived the lives of householders, with families and jobs, to take certain vows for one day. During that day they didn't eat after the noon meal and tried to maintain those vows to the best of their ability.

They could do this practice as often as they wished, but usually at least once a month.

In the appendix we have listed the vows taken by members of the Peacemaker Order. You might consider taking such vows for one day and examining your life with their help. It doesn't have to be these vows, it can be whatever rules and guidelines you use for your own life. The important thing is to take a day on some regular basis when you stop the important work you're doing and look at your life very personally and very intimately. For each vow or rule, ask yourself "What does this mean to me and how has my observance, or lack of observance, of this vow caused suffering for me and for others, who are no other than me?"

To make the task less overwhelming, we sometimes dedicate the Day of Reflection to one particular vow, bearing witness to our lives through that vow. Each vow is an instrument for looking at ourselves and listening to our own suffering.

I have been a social activist for many years. I've founded companies and organizations, developed training programs, and led many, many retreats. All these things are very important, and still I continue to be amazed by the healing power of listening. Listening without talk, without mental babble, without answers. Listening from unknowing. Think of those occasions in your life when something troubled you deeply and you recounted it to a family member or a friend who listened in this way. Such occasions are rare, for this kind of listening is very hard to come by. We try to teach it in our training programs. Sometimes all someone needs is to be listened to in this way.

When we bear witness to ourselves on the Day

of Reflection, we are listening to ourselves in that same deep, intimate way. We're not passing judgment, criticizing, or thinking about right or wrong. This act of unconditional listening and profound intimacy has tremendous healing power.

Try to listen to yourself using these or other vows. Make of it a day of practice. Don't be afraid to look at your issues. When we're on the streets we recite a service twice a day in which we offer the Supreme Meal to all the hungry spirits in the Ten Directions. In offering ourselves we offer a feast. We may not consider it a feast, or we may think it's a feast of imperfections. We offer our shyness, our anger, our love, our lust, our ignorance, our determination. Whatever you see in yourself, whatever you are, that's your offering.

And it's a banquet. You don't have to eat everything, you can pick what you need, pick what tastes good. Don't be so overwhelmed that you don't touch any of it. No matter how much you eat, there's always more. In fact, there's an abundance. So long as we offer ourselves, with all our ingredients, there's enough for everybody.

— 34 —

Telling Stories

The Zen Peacemaker Order is a place where peace-makers tell their stories.

This book is my story: my time on the streets, at Auschwitz, in School 6, in the order. It's a story of relationships: with my wife and cofounder, Jishu Holmes; with other peacemakers, associates, and students; and with the people who've been my greatest teachers these last years—the inhabitants of the Letten, the Bowery, Auschwitz—all of whom we've sewn into our order. It's the story of my own evolving life and practice.

I've been a Zen teacher for many years. Zen has a strong tradition of telling stories. In fact, many people first come to Zen because they read its koans, living tales of Chinese and Japanese Zen masters who say puzzling things and behave in outrageous ways. Zen is also known for its practice of silent meditation. This is not a harsh, repressive silence. When you do silent meditation you are not stopping the stories from coming up, the sun from shining, or the birds from singing. In fact, you bear witness to all the things that arise.

And I also know that certain silences don't help, they hurt. It's important to tell your story, to tell where it hurts. In the order, we call it talking meditation.

At Auschwitz, some people wanted to sit only

in silence. We had our times of silence, and we also chanted names. In chanting names we were telling stories of lives that went up in smoke. We recited thousands of names, thousands of stories. In that place it was important not to stay silent, not to aid forgetfulness. Each time we spoke a name we bore witness and gave life to dry bones.

My own spiritual training came out of a monastic model. In a Zen monastery, the environment is carefully, meticulously controlled to bring the monks to a state of unknowing and experiencing the oneness of life. But I chose not to live in a monastery. I got involved in business, social action, and peacemaking. So for me the question became, What are the forms in business, social action, and peacemaking that can help us see the oneness of society, the interdependence of life? My entire teaching life has been dedicated to creating new environments and structures, new business and social forms that will move each of us toward the realization and actualization of the enlightened way, which is nothing other than peacemaking.

Just doing silent meditation doesn't necessarily bring us there. So what else can we do? What are the methods, the expedient means? This is the challenge I face, day in, day out.

Telling stories is one way of doing this, for it's bearing witness. Without speaking the hurt, the healing won't come.

So although it's now summer, I'm looking back to a spring day three months ago. I'm sitting in my living room with Jishu and with Joan Halifax. It's mid-afternoon two months before Joan's ordination, and she is sewing her peacemaker robe. We're talking quietly because we're a little tired, while Joan, seated on the couch, is stitching piece after piece, panel after panel. The sunbeams dance on the fabrics. They're all beautiful. Even after being dipped in a dark dye, they've come out purple, magenta, rust, blue, and dark green. Even after death, people's lives are beautiful. As she sews the pieces, she recites names.

> The quilting piece is from Nina Crandall Linton, who died of heart problems.
> The pink dress is from Marge McCarthy, who survived breast cancer.
> This gown is mine, made by John Russell and Kenny Lichtman, who died of AIDS.
> Ken Ballard, who survived testicular cancer.
> Eunice Halifax, who hemorrhaged to death during surgery.
> Julia Rindler Kaufman.
> Patricia Lake.
> Robert Samson.

Joan will wear their stories on her body. Her robe is not black crepe or ashcloth, it's dazzling color.

> Bill Isaacs.
> Kathleen O'Rourke.
> Lana Lea Lasky-Beaseley.
> Art Lofton.

I hope that our work in the Zen Peacemaker Order will be known not so much for the work done in our Peacemaker Villages but for penetrating the unknown, letting go of what we know, and bearing witness to pain and joy in ourselves and in the universe. For telling our stories again and again.

Let me conclude with one final story.

Jishu and I went to visit Fleet Maull right after the New Year in 1996. We flew to California from our home in Yonkers, and then drove from Los Angeles to Springfield, Missouri. As soon as we saw Fleet we knew something had happened. Fleet told us that he'd just come out of the "hole." This was how it happened:

After two and a half years of living in large, crowded prison dormitories and sharing cells of various sizes with other prisoners, Fleet had finally obtained one of only two private cells available. This was a very valuable privilege, for it enabled him to do his work and practice in some quiet and privacy, rather than coping with the endless noise of shared cells and dormitories where the men played cards and dominoes, joked, and carried on. This private cell also allowed Fleet to do a nine-day solitary retreat each year during his allotted vacation time. He had kept it for eight years, no easy matter. Prison life has many rules, and with the slightest infraction he could lose the privacy that was so important to his work.

One of these rules is that five times a day prison guards do institutional counts, when they hand-count all inmates to make sure no one has disappeared. Each inmate has to stand by the bars to be counted during that time. A week before we'd arrived Fleet had gone to the bathroom to brush his teeth. When he returned to his cell he found that he'd missed the count. Immediately he was handcuffed and taken by the guards to the hole.

Going to the hole meant many things. It meant

an incident report, or "shot," on his record. It meant that guards bagged up the personal property in his room. Almost certainly, it meant that he would lose all his privileges, including his single room, and start all over again, on the top bunk of a twenty-six-man cell. Worst of all, Fleet had worked hard over the previous six months to put together a clemency petition to President Clinton asking for a commutation of the remainder of his sentence, and now he worried that he had let down the hundreds of people who had written letters and provided other assistance in support of the petition. Whereas once the accompanying progress report would have reflected no incidents, now it would report that he'd interfered with the security count and had been sent to the hole.

Some guards were sympathetic, assuring Fleet they would have never done this to him given his clean record for so many years. But one guard did, and it was enough.

Fleet spent three days in the hole. He didn't sleep the first night. He was heavily involved in the drama of what had happened, the unfairness of it all. Then, after doing his meditation practice, much of the pain dissolved and he could consider what had occurred with more clarity and equanimity.

On the third day his boss came by and told him that not only would he be getting out of the hole, but that the shot would be expunged. Various staff members were calling the correctional counsel trying to get him out. Fleet didn't believe it. He was sure that at the very least he would lose his private cell. But when he was released he found that the shot had indeed been expunged from his record, the cell was still his, and the clemency petition was still on track.

Nevertheless, this had not been easy. One moment of carelessness, one instant of inattention, and look what happened. Another guard might not have made such a fuss over it, but one did.

Life is a precarious thing. A slight moment of distraction, a tiny oversight, and everything turns. Suddenly the ground is ripped from under us; we lose our privileges, our homes, sometimes our lives. Because of a thoughtless word, an inattentive glance, someone coming to work in a bad mood.

What do we do? We do the best we can. I am going to die the very next instant, and the instant after that, and after that, so I am doing the best I can this instant. To say that everything is changing is to say that everything is going to die this very instant. So we must do the very best we can each moment, as if each moment were our last—because it is!

Appendix

PEACEMAKER VOWS FOR THE DAY OF REFLECTION

These are the peacemaker vows recited by members of the Zen Peacemaker Order on the Day of Reflection, which falls on the fourth Saturday of every month.

In the morning of the Day of Reflection, we recite the following:

I, _____, now recite the Verse of Atonement.

All evil karma ever committed by me since of old, on account of my beginningless greed, anger, and ignorance, born of my body, speech, and mind, now I atone for it all.

Now being mindful of the purity of my body, speech, and mind, I commit myself to observing this Day of Reflection with the following practices:

I, _____, for the coming day, take refuge in the Buddha, the awakened nature of all beings; in the Dharma, the ocean of wisdom and compassion; and in the Sangha, the community of those living in harmony with all Buddhas and Dharmas.

I, _____, for the coming day, commit myself to not-knowing, the source of all manifestations, and seeing all manifestations as the teachings of not-knowing; I further commit myself to bearing witness by allowing myself to be touched by the joys and pain of the universe; I invite all hungry spirits into the mandala of my being and commit my energy and my love to the healing of myself, the earth, humanity, and all creations.

1. As peacemakers, throughout all space and time, have observed the precept of non-killing; not leading a harmful life nor encouraging others to do so, so will I, _____, with gratitude, for the duration of one day, recognize that I am not separate from all that is. I will live in harmony with all life and the environment which sustains it.

2. As peacemakers, throughout all space and time, have observed the precept of non-stealing, so will I,_____,with contentment, for the duration of one day, be satisfied with what I have, I will freely give, ask for, and accept what is needed.

3. As peacemakers, throughout all space and time, have observed the precept of chaste conduct, so will I, _____ , with love, for the duration of one day, encounter all creations with respect and dignity. I will give and accept love and friendship without clinging.

4. As peacemakers, throughout all space and time, have observed the precept of non-lying; speaking the truth and deceiving no one, so will I,_____, with honesty, for the duration of one day, listen and speak from the heart. I will see and act in accordance with what is.

5. As peacemakers, throughout all space and time, have observed the precept of not being deluded, nor encouraged others to do so, so will I, _____, with awareness, for the duration of one day, cultivate a mind that sees clearly. I will embrace all experience directly.

6. As peacemakers, throughout all space and time, have observed the precept of not talking about others' errors and faults, so will I, _____, with kindness, for the duration of one day, unconditionally accept what each moment has to offer. I will acknowledge responsibility for everything in my life.

7. As peacemakers, throughout all space and time, have observed the precept of not elevating themselves and blaming others, so will I,_____, with humility, for the duration of one day, speak what I perceive to be the truth without guilt or blame. I will give my best effort and accept the results.

8. As peacemakers, throughout all space and time, have observed the precept of not being stingy, so will I,_____, with generosity, for the duration of one day, use all of the ingredients of my life. I will not foster a mind of poverty in myself or others.

9. As peacemakers, throughout all space and time, have observed the precept of not being angry, not harboring resentment, rage, or revenge, so will I,_____, with determination, for the duration of one day, transform suffering into wisdom. I will roll all negative experience into my practice.

10. As peacemakers, throughout all space and time, have observed the precept of not thinking ill of the

three treasures, so will I, _____, with compassion, for the duration of one day, honor my life as an instrument of peacemaking. I will recognize myself and others as manifestations of Oneness, Diversity, and Harmony.

I, _____, have committed myself to this peacemaker practice for the duration of one day. May the merits of this practice be extended to all those who dedicate their lives to the practice of peace and to all those who suffer from the oppression of my own greed, anger, and ignorance. I wish to transform the passions that afflict me and to realize and actualize the enlightened way through the practice of not-knowing, bearing witness, and healing.

ABOUT THE AUTHOR

Bernie Glassman is abbot of the Zen Community of New York, the Zen Center of Los Angeles, and Zen Mountain Center in Idyllwild, California. Along with his late wife, Jishu Holmes, he is the cofounder of the Zen Peacemaker Order, an international order of social activists engaged in peacemaking based on the Three Tenets: penetrating the unknown, bearing witness to joy and suffering, and healing ourselves and others.

Roshi Glassman is also the founder of the Greyston Mandala, a network of businesses and not-for-profits doing community development work in southwest Yonkers, New York. He is a former aerospace engineer who worked on manned missions to Mars at McDonnell-Douglas during the 1970s. He holds a Ph.D. in applied mathematics from UCLA. He trained in Zen Buddhism under Taizan Maezumi Roshi in Los Angeles.

If, after reading this book, you would like to know more about the Zen Peacemaker Order and its Peacemaker Villages, you may contact the order at Box 313, La Honda, CA 94020 or via E-mail at the following address: peacemaker@ibm.net. Or visit its website: www.peacemakercommunity.org

OTHER BELL TOWER BOOKS

Books that nourish the soul, illuminate the mind,
and speak directly to the heart

Valeria Alfeyeva
PILGRIMAGE TO DZHVARI
A Woman's Journey of Spiritual Awakening
An unforgettable introduction to the riches of the Eastern
Orthodox mystical tradition. A modern *Way of a Pilgrim.*
0-517-88389-9 Softcover

Madeline Bruser
THE ART OF PRACTICING
Making Music from the Heart
A classic work on how to practice music which combines
meditative principles with information on body mechanics
and medicine.
0-609-80177-5 Softcover

Melody Ermachild Chavis
ALTARS IN THE STREET
A Courageous Memoir of Community and Spiritual Awakening
A deeply moving account that captures the essence of
human struggles and resourcefulness.
0-609-80196-1 Softcover

Tracy Cochran and Jeff Zaleski
TRANSFORMATIONS
Awakening to the Sacred in Ourselves
An exploration of enlightenment experiences and
the ways in which they can transform our lives.
0-517-70150-2 Hardcover

David A. Cooper
ENTERING THE SACRED MOUNTAIN
Exploring the Mystical Practices of Judaism,
Buddhism, and Sufism
An inspiring chronicle of one man's search for truth.
0-517-88464-X Softcover

Marc David
NOURISHING WISDOM
A Mind/Body Approach to Nutrition and Well-Being
A book that advocates awareness in eating.
0-517-88129-2 Softcover

Kat Duff
THE ALCHEMY OF ILLNESS
A luminous inquiry into the function and purpose of illness.
0-517-88097-0 Softcover

Joan Furman, MSN, RN, and David McNabb
THE DYING TIME
Practical Wisdom for the Dying and Their Caregivers
A comprehensive guide, filled with physical, emotional,
and spiritual advice.
0-609-80003-5 Softcover

Bernard Glassman and Rick Fields
INSTRUCTIONS TO THE COOK
A Zen Master's Lessons in Living a Life That Matters
A distillation of Zen wisdom that can be used equally well as
a manual on business or spiritual practice, cooking or life.
0-517-88829-7 Softcover

Burghild Nina Holzer
A WALK BETWEEN HEAVEN AND EARTH
A Personal Journal on Writing and the Creative Process
How keeping a journal focuses and expands our awareness
of ourselves and everything that touches our lives.
0-517-88096-2 Softcover

Greg Johanson and Ron Kurtz
GRACE UNFOLDING
Psychotherapy in the Spirit of the Tao-te ching
The interaction of client and therapist illuminated through the
gentle power and wisdom of Lao Tsu's ancient classic.
0-517-88130-6 Softcover

Selected by Marcia and Jack Kelly
ONE HUNDRED GRACES
Mealtime Blessings
A collection of graces from many traditions,
inscribed in calligraphy reminiscent of the manuscripts of
medieval Europe.
0-517-58567-7 Hardcover
0-609-80093-0 Softcover

Jack and Marcia Kelly
SANCTUARIES
*A Guide to Lodgings in Monasteries, Abbeys, and Retreats
of the United States*
For those in search of renewal and a little peace;
described by the *New York Times* as "the *Michelin Guide*
of the retreat set."
0-517-88517-4 Softcover

Marcia and Jack Kelly
THE WHOLE HEAVEN CATALOG
*A Resource Guide to Products, Services, Arts, Crafts,
and Festivals of Religious, Spiritual, and
Cooperative Communities*
All the things that monks and nuns do to support their habits!
0-609-80120-1 Softcover

Marcia M. Kelly
HEAVENLY FEASTS
Memorable Meals from Monasteries, Abbeys, and Retreats
Thirty-nine celestial menus from the more than 250
monasteries the Kellys have visited on their travels.
0-517-88522-0 Softcover

Barbara Lachman
THE JOURNAL OF HILDEGARD OF BINGEN
A year in the life of the twelfth-century German saint—
the diary she never had the time to write herself.
0-517-88390-2 Softcover

Katharine Le Mée
CHANT
The Origins, Form, Practice, and Healing Power
of Gregorian Chant
The ways in which this ancient liturgy can nourish us and
transform our lives.
0-517-70037-9 Hardcover

Stephen Levine
A YEAR TO LIVE
How to Live This Year as if It Were Your Last
Using the consciousness of our mortality
to enter into a new and vibrant relationship with life.
0-609-80194-5 Softcover

Gunilla Norris
BEING HOME
A Book of Meditations
An exquisite modern book of hours,
a celebration of mindfulness in everyday activities.
0-517-58159-0 Hardcover

Marcia Prager
THE PATH OF BLESSING
Experiencing the Energy and Abundance of the Divine
How to use the traditional Jewish practice of calling down a
blessing on each action as a profound path of spiritual growth.
0-517-70363-7 Hardcover

Ram Dass and Mirabai Bush
COMPASSION IN ACTION
Setting Out on the Path of Service
Heartfelt encouragement and advice for those ready to commit
time and energy to relieving suffering in the world.
0-517-88500-X Softcover

Saki Santorelli
HEAL THY SELF
Lessons on Mindfulness in Medicine
An invitation to patients and health care professionals to bring
mindfulness into the crucible of the healing relationship.
0-609-60385-X Hardcover

Rabbi Rami M. Shapiro
MINYAN
Ten Principles for Living a Life of Integrity
A primer for those interested to know what Judaism has to
offer the spiritually hungry.
0-609-80055-8 Softcover

Rabbi Rami M. Shapiro
WISDOM OF THE JEWISH SAGES
A Modern Reading of Pirke Avot
A third-century treasury of maxims on justice, integrity, and
virtue—Judaism's principal ethical scripture.
0-517-79966-9 Hardcover

James Thornton
A FIELD GUIDE TO THE SOUL
A Down-to-Earth Handbook of Spiritual Practice
A manual for coming into harmony and communion
with the earth.
0-609-60368-X Hardcover

Joan Tollifson
BARE-BONES MEDITATION

Waking Up from the Story of My Life

An unvarnished, exhilarating account of one woman's struggle
to make sense of her life.

0-517-88792-4 Softcover

Michael Toms and Justine Willis Toms
TRUE WORK

Doing What You Love and Loving What You Do

Wisdom for the workplace from the husband-and-wife team
of NPR's weekly radio program *New Dimensions*.

0-609-80212-7 Softcover

BUDDHA LAUGHING

A Tricycle Book of Cartoons

A marvelous opportunity for self-reflection
for those who tend to take themselves too seriously.

0-609-80409-X Softcover

Ed. Richard Whelan
SELF-RELIANCE

*The Wisdom of Ralph Waldo Emerson
as Inspiration for Daily Living*

A distillation of Emerson's spiritual writings
for contemporary readers.

0-517-58512-X Softcover

*Bell Tower books are for sale at your local bookstore
or you may call Random House at 1-800-793-BOOK to order with
a credit card.*